The New Information Professional

CHANDOS
INFORMATION PROFESSIONAL SERIES

Series Editor: Ruth Rikowski
(email: rikowski@tiscali.co.uk)

Chandos' new series of books are aimed at the busy information professional. They have been specially commissioned to provide the reader with an authoritative view of current thinking. They are designed to provide easy-to-read and (most importantly) practical coverage of topics that are of interest to librarians and other information professionals. If you would like a full listing of current and forthcoming titles, please visit our web site **www.chandospublishing.com** or contact Hannah Grace-Williams on email info@chandospublishing.com or telephone number +44 (0) 1865 884447.

New authors: we are always pleased to receive ideas for new titles; if you would like to write a book for Chandos, please contact Dr Glyn Jones on email gjones@chandospublishing.com or telephone number +44 (0)1865 884447.

Bulk orders: some organisations buy a number of copies of our books. If you are interested in doing this, we would be pleased to discuss a discount. Please contact Hannah Grace-Williams on email info@chandospublishing.com or telephone number +44 (0) 1865 884447.

The New Information Professional

How to thrive in the Information Age doing what you love

SUE MYBURGH

Chandos Publishing
Oxford · England

Chandos Publishing (Oxford) Limited
Chandos House
5 & 6 Steadys Lane
Stanton Harcourt
Oxford OX29 5RL
UK
Tel: +44 (0) 1865 884447 Fax: +44 (0) 1865 884448
Email: info@chandospublishing.com
www.chandospublishing.com

First published in Great Britain in 2005

ISBN:
1 84334 087 9 (paperback)
1 84334 097 6 (hardback)

© Sue Myburgh, 2005

British Library Cataloguing-in-Publication Data.
A catalogue record for this book is available from the British Library.

Cover images courtesy of Bytec Solutions Ltd (*www.bytecweb.com*) and David Hibberd (*DAHibberd@aol.com*).

Printed in the UK and USA.

To my children, Trixie and Carl, for their patience and humour.

To my mother, Betty Collins, for getting me into this in the first place.

Contents

List of abbreviations

AACR2	Anglo-American Cataloguing Rules, 2nd edn
ALARM	Alliance of Libraries, Archives and Records Managers
ALISE	Association for Library and Information Science Education
ANT	actor-network theory
ARPANET	Advanced Research Projects Agency Network (US Department of Defense)
ASIST	American Society of Information Science and Technology
ASK	'anomalous states of knowledge' (Belkin, 1980)
CI	competitive intelligence
DDC	Dewey Decimal Classification System
FOI	freedom of information
HIB	human information behaviour
HSS	Humanities and Social Sciences
IA	information architecture
ICT	information and communication technology
IFLA	International Federation of Library Associations and Institutions
IP	information professional
IM	information management
IPAC	Information Policy Advisory Council (Australia)
IR	information retrieval
IRM	information resources management
IS	Information Society
IT	information technology

KALIPER	Kellogg-ALISE Information Professions and Education Reform Project
KM	knowledge management
LCSH	Library of Congress Subject Headings
LIS	library and information science
MDG	Millennium Development Goal
MST	'Meta-System Transition' (Turchin, 1977)
NS	Natural Sciences
RTO	Registered Training Organisation (Australia)
SCOT	social construction of technology
SE	social epistemology
SDI	selective dissemination of information
SI	social informatics
SIM	strategic information management
STP	socio-technical perspective
SST	social shaping of technology
TD	technological determinism
TIPs	traditional information professions
WSIS	World Summit on the Information Society

Preface

Librarians and other information professionals, such as records managers, archivists and museum curators, have long been taken for granted as the almost invisible, but nonetheless omnipresent and indispensable, guardians of the record of human thought, creation, discovery and invention. While storehouses of recorded information and informational artefacts have existed since the time of the cuneiform-inscribed clay tablets of the Sumerian civilisation, the professions have only fairly recently – in the past few centuries – been differentiated, largely by the institution in which the profession is practised, by the clientele served or by the type of document or artefact housed and managed in the institution.

Variations in professional theory and practice have been emphasised by professionals and their professional associations, and this has resulted in increasing heterogony in practice, terminology, objectives, standards and tools. Continuing diversification and specialisation do not necessarily indicate a flaw in the growth of a profession: probably the contrary. However, the onslaught of rapid changes, led by revolutions in computer and communications technologies combined with constant ongoing social change, have wrought modifications and transformations in most fields of human endeavour, and these changes have demanded a response from those who manage information, and the documents and artefacts that contain or represent it.

Discerning an adequate response to these environmental changes from the information professions is extraordinarily complex. The growth of human knowledge, and the concomitant growth in records representing such knowledge, has not been confined to any one discipline, topic or subject area. Knowledge creation and information communication form the foundation of every human endeavour, from fishing to space exploration: knowledge and information are constantly accreting, changing, developing. Information flows and containers are not discipline specific: neither is managing them.

Until the rapid development of information and communication technologies (ICTs) in the last few decades, little distinction was made between data, information and knowledge. Documents, such as books, were regarded as synonymous with information and knowledge; as computers developed, it was understood that what they did was compute data. The information explosion was often described in terms of the number of journals or monographs published within a particular year, and this appeared to be a most satisfactory explanation.

While information was contained exclusively in physical documents, information professionals could be said to be information managers in so far as they had physical control over these items. Librarians, records managers and archivists were indisputably and visibly the gatekeepers to the kingdom of information, learning and knowledge creation. Furthermore, their role was a noble one, a social service which could transform the uneducated into the educated, the poor into the rich, the miserable and lonely into the entertained, the rough and non-productive into cultured and useful citizens and workers.

However, the ICTs fundamentally changed all three of the basic pillars upon which the information professions rest: the containers of information, i.e. the documents themselves, the means by which they can be communicated and the tools used to manage them. Documents have become invisible, as all information, whether text, graphics, video or sound, can now be captured digitally; digital transmission of information contained in documents has been made possible using existing telephone lines and, more recently, fibre-optic cable; and tools such as catalogues, which were in effect manual databases of metadata used to control and provide access to document collections, have been easily computerised and expanded to provide full-text access.

Easy, cheap and individual publication, communication and access to information has now become the norm in most parts of the developed world, and this has led to a reconsideration of the role of information in education, commerce, science, entertainment and many other areas, so much so that individuals, organisations, nations and the United Nations itself have been forced to consider their own information conduct, behaviour and policies. The creation or production of knowledge, and the possession of information, are considered economic indicators related to power, prosperity and peace. New areas are being examined and developed: intellectual property and knowledge management, the digital divide and privacy, surveillance and competitive advantage – all are related to the digital capture and transmission of information.

Because of the prominence and perceived value of information, many new players have been attracted to the information 'industry'. These include, of course, the technologists – those who develop and construct hardware and software, and those who install and maintain it for effective use. In addition, information is a primary concern, or even stock-in-trade, of accountants, economists, development agencies, educators and others, apart from the general reliance of all human activity on information, as noted previously. New players are also found in those areas of information management which have been ignored or underdeveloped by the traditional information professions: corporate and strategic information management, knowledge management, competitive intelligence, information architecture on the Web and so on. Many of these practitioners have no background in the traditional information professions, even though, ironically, these are frequently precisely the skills that are required.

So far, the response to these technological changes from the traditional information professions has been patchy and partial. Information institutions, such as libraries and archives, have concentrated on the incorporation of information technologies to support, and sometimes expand, existing practices. This has focused attention on information professionals acquiring technical skills. Some changes facilitated by ICTs are regarded as threats as information professionals lose control – users searching the Internet independently of an information intermediary are seen as a threat rather than an opportunity to play a different role – while at the same time the construction of sophisticated databases describing literature in specific fields rather than specific libraries, as well as information retrieval tools such as search engines have been passively relinquished to the technologists. As a result, the traditional information professionals are seen by many (outside of the professions themselves) as redundant, while the professionals themselves argue that their knowledge base is central to the development of the Information Society.

There are several reasons why the traditional information professions are, in many ways, marginalised by contemporary society. Among these, issues such as the feminisation of the professions, their leaning towards literature and high culture, the model of the public library as a social agency for upliftment and the focus on place as the venue for professional practice have been mentioned by several writers. However, the confusion between information, knowledge and documents, and the practicable distinctions between these concepts, has meant that the traditional information professions lack fundamental theory to support their practice: a theory which could help interpret changing technologies and the application of professional knowledge to changing information problems. At the same time, such a theory would connect the information professions in a meaningful way that would clearly demarcate professional territory and clarify for users what information professionals can do.

It is argued here that the traditional information professionals have concentrated on document management and the management of warehouses of documents, and that they have not been managing information at all. Indeed, according to the definitions offered in this work, no profession has in fact been managing information itself, as documents, libraries and information can no longer be regarded as synonymous.

The traditional information professions are under threat in a number of areas. Information work itself is poorly understood even by information professionals themselves as it is predicated upon document management, and this has given rise to a number of myths that surround the nature of information work, providing a paradigm of the discipline which is riddled with anomalies. While the traditional information professions continue to operate only within the confines of their habitus, displaying predispositions and habits which constrain development, solutions to this paradoxical dilemma will not be determined.

It was mentioned above that information is fundamental to all areas of human activity: this would imply that information management likewise should be multidisciplinary.

Both multi- and interdisciplinary perspectives are required in order to manage information effectively.

The knowledge base of the information discipline, like other disciplines such as physics, could also experience a Kuhnian paradigm shift once a sufficient number of anomalies have accrued. The prevalent information discourse has been shaped by social events, institutions and practices that, by and large, no longer exist. Postmodernism suggests that different interpretations of information and its management are possible; new knowledge in the information discipline can be created in what Gibbons et al. (1994) have called Mode 2 – a fluid, contextualised, heterogenous interdisciplinary approach which considers new ways of examining societal information problems.

Adopting this approach will assist the traditional information professions to understand and respond to the changes in their environment in order to respond appropriately and even proactively create change. The role of the information professions in the Information Society, in particular their social and political role, may be better understood and developed. While, on the one hand, the development of a core metatheory applicable to all information professions is seen as desirable, it is also stressed that, like professions such as medicine and law, specialisation will nonetheless be required as there are many types of information work.

This work comprises an individual effort, although it has obviously been supported by the numerous authors who have worked in this, and adjacent, areas. With that said, it is recognised that there is still a great deal of work to be done which is beyond the abilities of a lone researcher. Thus I will be satisfied if I have done little else other than to begin a debate.

Foreword

Not many studies reflect analytically on the identity of the information professions and the work of information professionals. And those that are theoretically grounded are rare. Sue Myburgh's monograph is therefore a special contribution to the professional literature.

Newness in information work has lost much of its meaning in the welter of fashionable terms used to express what has really been around for a long time. There are regular announcements of new techniques and tools that upon examination turn out to be little more than 'old wine in new bottles'. On the other hand, there is a cyclical renewal of serious interest in philosophical aspects of information work. We are currently witnessing such a renewal. But the challenge is how to apply these ideas in order to secure a credible foundation for the information professions.

This requires an integrated or holistic outlook favoured by the kind of thinkers who can supply a theoretical foundation for what Myburgh calls a metacommunity of new information professionals. She presents an attractive way of how this can be achieved, and skilfully avoids setting up traditional information professions as a foil for describing the new information professional.

Instead, the argument that changing circumstances and challenges both push and pull the information professions to evolve in another direction is convincing. I am certain that this book will help shift thinking about information professionals in a new direction.

Archie L. Dick
Pretoria, South Africa

About the author

Sue Myburgh was born in Cape Town, South Africa, and educated at the University of Cape Town and the University of South Africa. Her working experience in the area of information management has been diverse, including public, academic and corporate libraries, undertaking cataloguing and reference work, online database searching, acquisitions, serials control and records management, as well as consultancies and freelance indexing and abstracting.

Awarded a Fulbright Fellowship in 1982 to study at Simmons College in Boston, Massachusetts, Sue has been an academic since 1984, and has written numerous articles in the areas of education for library and information science, records and strategic information management, knowledge management and gender and technology. She is frequently invited to speak at international conferences, often as keynote speaker. She is also a reviewer for, or on the editorial board of, several professional journals, and has served on several conference programme committees.

Sue has been awarded several honours and awards besides the Fulbright, including the Silver Jubilee Prize at the University of Cape Town and the Britt Literary Award from the Association of Records Managers and Administrators (ARMA) International. She serves on several professional committees, and is currently International Ambassador (Australasia) for ARMA International.

Sue has had a long-standing interest in curriculum development for the education and training of information professionals, with particular emphasis on addressing their changing cultural, societal and organisational roles. Her current research interests include information-seeking behaviour and information use, particularly in organisational environments. Her career in academia spans two decades, and she is currently a senior academic at the University of South Australia where she teaches in the areas of information retrieval, record-keeping, knowledge representation and strategic information management.

The author may be contacted via the publishers.

The end is nigh – long live the end

Unless there is better understanding of the theoretical structure of the traditional information professions (TIPs), their practice is doomed.

While there remains a range of opinion concerning what information is, there is consensus that this should be the primary focus for the TIPs, but in the contemporary context of the training of information professionals, the emphasis is still on document management. Traditional information professionals (IPs) may actually be unable to understand the role of information in today's society. At the same time, the TIPs stand poised at a threshold, beyond which lies an opportunity to play a significant role in the Information Society (IS), assisting individuals and organisations to reap the benefits of useful information.

Any profession is reliant upon a core body of knowledge outlining and governing its practices, as is made clear for instance in this definition from the Australian Council of Professions:

> 'Profession' means a disciplined group of individuals who adhere to high ethical standards and uphold themselves to, and are accepted by, the public as possessing special knowledge and skills in a widely recognised, organised body of learning derived from education and training at a high level and who are prepared to exercise this knowledge and these skills in the interests of others. (Australian Council of Professions, 2003)

Parsons holds that 'the boundaries of the group system we generally call the professions are fluid and indistinct'; he suggests that there are several core criteria which distinguish professional work from the work of other occupations, namely a 'requirement of formal technical training ... giving prominence to an *intellectual* component'; the development of 'skills in some form of its use'; and the 'socially responsible uses' of the profession (Parsons, 1968).

Few would disagree with this. Professions are distinguished by the societal problems they address, the knowledge they possess in order to deal with these problems and the skills which are used to apply their knowledge. As a result, most professions share certain sets of beliefs. The goals to be pursued and the tools, methods and service models they use both follow and reinforce these ideas and ideals.

Abbott (1998) states clearly that a profession's strongest claim of jurisdiction over a problem is that its knowledge system is effective in the task domain, which Blackler (1995) compares to a 'blackbox' of professional knowledge. This professional knowledge is not shared by other professions: such isolation gives authority to such knowledge (Blackler, 1995). It is, however, precisely this practised and practicable 'knowledge' that is either indeterminate or lacking in the information professions. The problem is made particularly complex by recognising that, in the information professions, there is now a variety of task domains, making it particularly difficult to establish what the core knowledge system is.

Why is the Information Society just passing TIPs by?

This lack of a core identity of the information professions, among themselves and in the popular mind, has marginalised these professions in an era when, paradoxically, their role could be regarded as essential and central. There is a growing suspicion among the TIPs that, even though this is the IS, it is somehow all passing them by.

The chief characteristic of this society is the emphasis on the production, communication and use of information (Castells, 1996, 1997, 1998). Predominant features include a dramatic increase in the amount of information communicated in a variety of ways, and the ubiquitous use of information and communication technologies (ICTs) which facilitate such communication.

For many, the IS is symbolised by the Internet, which is enigmatically surrounded by hyperbole and obfuscation yet at heart is a digitised communications medium for all modes of information storage and exchange. Across this complex platform, increasing numbers of documents are being generated, and there are unprecedented communication options. Yet, at the same time, individuals and organisations are losing the ability to manage, interpret and act on relevant information.

Besides the incorporation of new tools of technology into traditional activities, there are wider cultural and economic implications arising from the use of ICTs. Such phenomena as the IS, the Knowledge Economy, e-commerce and globalisation have led to an unprecedented interest in information by governments and even the United Nations. Traditional information professionals are only peripherally involved at this level of policy formation, and continue to have little, if any, input in major debates concerning how and why people use information, issues surrounding privacy, the development of organisational or national information policy, the costing of information products and the slew of issues associated with Internet activities.

TIPs believe that they could make a significant contribution to the central processes, issues and debates of the IS, but paradoxically librarians, record-keepers and archivists, habituated to being the custodians of information, are not prominent in the information industry and do not receive recognition for their knowledge and expertise. Instead of acting as gatekeepers of information about information, there are many challenges facing the traditional IPs, threatening to submerge them completely. Some of these challenges are listed below.

Competition from other professions

■ Accountants, computer scientists and information system managers are taking over TIP territory.

■ New IPs, such as knowledge management (KM), competitive intelligence (CI), strategic information management (SIM) and information architecture (IA) have developed to fill the gaps left by the TIPs and do the kinds of information work that is required by organisations.[1]

■ What is worse, the newcomers appear better able to meet the many challenges that arise in the complex, knowledge-based networked environment in which we live and work.

The future role of librarians and libraries

■ There seems to be a lack of consensus about whether libraries and librarianship, records management and even archives will survive at all, and if so, what role they will play in the future.

■ Information work itself is changing – there are shifts from permanence to transience in both documents and employment, and pressure to offer customised instead of generic services.

- The career paths of young practitioners are becoming increasingly fragmented, long-term experience in a single job setting is becoming rare and opportunities for induction programmes based on apprentice–mentor training are diminishing.

- There is increasingly easy access to global information resources, leading to disintermediation as information users work directly with information management systems, questioning the need for information intermediaries.

- Virtuality, digital libraries and digital preservation mean that in addition to disintermediation there is the notion of postcustodiality, which suggests that traditional IPs, as custodians of warehouses of documents, will become increasingly redundant or, at the very least, will need to change their role in the virtual world.

- Traditional work is less frequently available to new graduates, as constantly diminishing public funding means that jobs in large public, academic and school library systems stay static or diminish over time, while new graduates wait for the greying of the profession.[2]

The changing environment

- ICTs affect the ways in which communication takes place, and thus change the nature and fabric of societies and organisations. These changes are poorly understood by traditional IPs.

- Globalisation is facilitated by ICTs, which means an awareness of international practices is increasingly essential, but lacking. There is concomitant mobility of individuals as well.

- There are problems with keeping up with developing and obsolescing technologies.

- Traditional IPs find that their work is increasingly being taken over by information technologists, who are generally unaware of the responsibilities and specialised functions of IPs.

- Information is increasingly regarded as a commodity, with associated strategic, economic and competitive dimensions.

Loss of skills and knowledge base

- Traditional IPs no longer make the tools which assist in managing information, having given up responsibility for the creation of thesauri and indexes which assist in finding information – knowledge representation and indexing have been done for some time, for the larger commercial concerns, by computer scientists and IT.

- Using information management tools is becoming increasingly disintermediated: users have direct access, with no information intermediary to assist in searching, filtering or sense-making. They are left increasingly to fend for themselves after short courses in 'information literacy', which usually comprise an introduction to specialised tools.

- Some areas of information management are becoming ubiquitous, such as file structures, web page marking up and design, and e-mail management, which are now the transparent skills required by every literate person.

- The invasion of TIP territory by 'rival' information groups is often bedevilled by the phenomenon of the reinvention of the wheel (albeit with different nomenclature).

Gender issues

- The TIPs are largely feminised professions based in the humanities which use qualitative research methodologies; they are under threat from the masculinised IT professions which are based in the sciences and use quantitative research methodologies.

- Traditional IPs are usually 'women with a mission', as described by Neill, who 'devote their efforts to enrich the lives of people though the reading of the great literary works' (Neill, 1991: 153). This selfless devotion to service and helping others contributes to the low public profile of TIPs, as typically feminised work is invisible and taken for granted (like housekeeping).

Education for the professions

- There is a lack of leadership from academia, aggravated by cognitive dissonance between academics and employers regarding the aims of professional education. There is conflict between the achievement of graduate level scholarship and research to develop the body of theory which advances the profession, and satisfying employers who pay most attention to introductory-level skills and competencies.

- Too much discussion takes place on what is core when we should be looking at the boundaries.

- There is a lack of credibility within universities that the IPs constitute an academic discipline in their own right, largely due to misunderstood identity and the perception that they are academically inferior, lack theory and research, and emphasise the acquisition of practical skills and competency-based outcomes. The TIP area is referred to as an 'academic impostor' (Manley, 1991: 70).

■ Senior library and information science (LIS) researchers are not regarded as community or opinion leaders in the IS, in areas such as information ethics, information economics and ICT use for social change.

■ There are increasing demands by social institutions on professional, applied disciplines to justify their existence and relevance related to perceived social needs.

■ Constant changes of identity and nomenclature have eroded public understanding of what the area is about.

■ The educational needs and skill sets of practitioners are rapidly changing due to the increasing specialisation of knowledge and the fast pace of technological development, but the areas covered in a first professional qualification have become more diffuse rather than focused on a specific and useful knowledge base.

■ Educational programmes in the traditional information areas have closed down (particularly in the United States, but also in Australia and elsewhere).

■ There is an increased need to access extra-disciplinary knowledge and to engage in meaningful transdisciplinary activities to address the problems of the IS, but this is seldom evident in TIP education programmes.

■ Static disciplinary boundaries and institutional frameworks are now impediments to developing the critical knowledge and creative approaches needed to solve complex information problems.

■ There are problems with accreditation as different educational organisations enter the market (such as the Registered Training Organisations (RTOs) in Australia)

and the increasing commercialisation of tertiary education, as well as the entrepreneurial approach infusing
traditional institutions of higher education.

- There is a lack of international reciprocity in the recognition of professional education programmes.
- Debates occur over the level and structure of programmes
for entry-level professional qualifications.
- The ageing population of TIPs means that more students
should enter into information management programmes
in order to sustain existing staff levels.

While these, and other, challenges have been debated in the
literature for some time, few radical or novel solutions have
been reached. Whether this is because of the innately conservative nature of the TIPs, fear of losing accreditation from
often rather conservative professional associations, lack of
funding for the research required, the lack of cohesiveness of
the professional area as a whole or a combination of all these
factors, is not clear. What is evident, however, is that there is
a sense that reformation is required which goes beyond attempts to redefine the image of the professions through
public relations and marketing. A re-examination of the
goals and objectives of the TIPs in terms of the societal needs
to which they need to respond and a definition and
description of the professional knowledge that is required to
undertake this role are required. Basic to these activities is
achieving conceptual clarity, cutting through the semantic
confusion that exists with regard to librarianship, information management, information science and, in particular,
core terms such as 'information', 'knowledge' and 'documents'.

The title of this chapter was chosen to indicate that the
TIPs might be coming to the end of the world as they know

it, but simultaneously, this closing provides an opportunity for radical reassessment and redefinition which will probably be necessary for some time. As somebody once said, 'We are not retreating. We are advancing in another direction'.

Notes

1. Many new jobs in the information industry have emerged which are not 'owned' by any profession (Willard and Mychalyn, 1998). 'The term *emerging [information] market* has been defined as "the employment opportunities available in information work that exist outside traditional libraries and information service units" and which use skills gained through LIS education' (Willard and Mychalyn, 1998: 316). This can even include records management and archival work.
2. See, for example, Kaye (2000) and Alderman (2001).

What is information work anyway?

So what is information work, and who are the information professionals? Anomalies and differences in the understanding of what information management is and how it is practised have led to a shocking lack of understanding – especially in government and business – of the various roles of information professionals. The definitions discussed below, rather than clarifying the matter, provide good reasons why this is so.

Sources of confusion

When the standard dictionary definitions of terms such as 'library' and 'librarian' are examined, not to mention 'information science' and other such phrases, it comes as no surprise that both professionals and the public at large might suffer some bewilderment with regard to what they actually do, particularly in a digital environment.

Webster's defines a **librarian** as 'a specialist in the care and management of a library'. Let us not forget that 'librarian' is derived from *liber*, the Latin for 'book'. With documents increasingly lacking physicality, managing a library, or any other storeroom of documents, becomes a more complicated process. Other definitions include 'one who copies manuscript books' and 'a professional person trained in library science and engaged in library services'. Last of all there is a definition which includes information: 'one who acquires, classifies, and facilitates access to information'.

A **library** is described as a 'collection of books kept for use' or a 'collection of literary documents or records kept for reference or borrowing'. A library is also a 'building for holding such a collection of books'. Once again, this notion is complicated in the virtual world and makes no provision for information services.

Librarianship is the practice of the profession. One definition holds that:

> Library science is distinct from librarianship, which is the practical *services* rendered by librarians in their day-to-day attempt to meet the needs of library patrons. Librarianship tends not to create new knowledge, nor to strive to advance any field or discipline. Librarians only rarely engage in library science, and then usually outside their jobs as librarians. But the study of library science is part of the requisite training of librarians.

It is clear from these definitions that librarianship focuses on the management of documents within specific warehouses as part of a cooperative relationship with a given community which requires such documents to be available, and where the acquisition and management of the required collection of documents is beyond the capacity of any one individual. It is also clear that librarianship involves the application, rather than the development, of professional knowledge. In this regard, librarianship can be regarded as a collection of applied, technical skills.

Library science (which, according to the definition given above, is what one has to study in order to become a librarian) '... includes academic studies (most often surveys) about how library resources are used and how people interact with library systems. These studies tend to be specific to certain libraries at certain times. The organization of knowledge for efficient retrieval of relevant information is also a major research goal ...' This brief description suggests a curriculum including acquisition, library user studies, classification and information retrieval; library science thus looks at document warehouse use and the use of document management systems.

Information science, on the other hand, is seen as a 'technical, cognitive, social and situational process', and Kando (1994) defines information science as being 'specifically concerned with information in the context of human communication'. However, Schrader, who studied about 700 definitions of 'information science' from 1900 to 1981 found that:

> ... the literature of information science is characterized by conceptual chaos. This conceptual chaos issues from a variety of problems in the definitional literature of information science: uncritical citing of previous definitions; conflating of study and practice; obsessive claims to scientific status; a narrow view of technology; disregard for literature without the science or technology label; inappropriate analogies; circular definition; and, the multiplicity of vague, contradictory, and sometimes bizarre notions of the nature of the term 'information'. (Schrader, 1983: 99)

The phrase **'information studies'** is plagued by a similar lack of understanding of the object of study – information – as this word itself is surrounded by conceptual and semantic confusion.

When library science and information science are put together, they become **library and information science (LIS)**, defined as 'the study of issues related to libraries' (although what these are is seldom fully expressed) and there is some argument that LIS is more appropriate than separate sciences of 'library' and 'information'. The emphasis on science is an interesting notion, which is also explored in more detail below. It is not easy to differentiate library studies from library science, as they both appear to focus on the library as the object of study.

There are frequent warnings that LIS cannot be confused with **information theory**, which is considered to be

> a branch of the mathematical theory of probability and mathematical statistics that quantifies the concept of information. It is concerned with information entropy, communication systems, data transmission and distortion, data compression and related topics. (*Wikipedia*, 2004)

There is no mention of libraries or librarianship. Information theory appears to have nothing to do with IPs according to this explanation.

It is generally believed that the modern discipline of information theory began with the publication of Shannon's article *The Mathematical Theory of Communication* (Shannon, 1948; Weaver and Shannon, 1949). Even though he is known primarily for this work in the field of communication, he expressly excluded from his model the issues of semantics and meaning and concentrated on the physical transmission of information, as emphasised in this quote by Borgmann:

> When Claude Shannon wrote his seminal article on information theory, he was concerned to keep the problem he had set himself crisp and clear. So he restricted himself to the structure of signs and explicitly

disregarded the question of what those signs might be about. He was interested in signals, not in the messages they were intended to convey. *'These semantic aspects of communication,'* Shannon said, *'are irrelevant to the engineering problem'* (Borgmann, 1999: 179, added emphasis)

When we take a look at record-keeping, we see the same emphasis on document management rather than information management. **Record-keeping** is defined as the 'making and maintaining of complete, accurate and reliable evidence of business transactions in the form of recorded information'. Records management and archives are essentially two points on the same continuum, as the following definition from the *Australian Standard* illustrates:

> Recordkeeping includes: the creation of records in the course of business activity and the means to ensure the creation of adequate records; the design, establishment and operation of recordkeeping systems; and the management of records used in business (traditionally regarded as the domain of records management) and as archives (traditionally regarded as the domain of archives administration). Adapted from *Standards Australia*, AS 4390, Part 1, Clause 4.19; AS 4390, Part 3, Foreword. (*Australian Glossary of Recordkeeping Terms*)

A **records manager** or records administrator is 'responsible for the administration of programmes for the efficient and economical handling, protecting, and disposing of records throughout their lifecycle', and **records management** is seen as

> The field of management responsible for the efficient and systematic control of the creation, receipt, maintenance, use and disposal of records, including processes for capturing and maintaining evidence of and

> information about business activities and transactions in the form of records. (Adapted from *Standards Australia*, AS ISO 15489, Part 1, Clause 3.16)

The emphasis is on maintaining the integrity of the document rather than the information it contains. An **archivist** is 'an individual responsible for appraising, acquiring, arranging, describing, preserving, and providing access to records of enduring value, according to the principles of provenance, original order, and collective control to protect the materials' authenticity and context', although they may need to become involved in records management at any stage of its lifecycle.

There are some international differences in this definition. In the United States, archivists are typically associated with collections of inactive records. However, the European tradition includes management of active records as well, which in the United States is often the responsibility of a separate records manager.

The generic term **information professional,** however, is often used as a synonym for librarian, although it is also used by various other groups, including records managers and computer scientists. However, public perception will not necessarily change with nomenclature unless the meaning of such a change can be understood.

Information management is also a term used by a range of practitioners, yet once more there is little consensus on what it actually means, largely due to the misunderstanding of the term 'information' and its frequent confusion with the concepts of 'data' and 'knowledge'. The ninth edition of *Harrod's Librarians' Glossary* defines information management as

> An imprecise term for the various activities that contribute to the effective production, co-ordination,

storage, retrieval and dissemination of information, in whatever format, and from internal and external sources, leading to the more efficient functioning of the organisation.

Bent's definition describes the most widely understood functions of IM:

> ... the enterprise-wide planning, organizing, directing, training, and controlling associated with organizational information. IM includes the management of various information resources: carriers of information such as documents or electronic media; departments which provide information services; and both computer-based or traditional information systems. (Bent, 1995)

Holtham and other writers have argued strongly that there is a need to emphasise the management of information itself rather than the technology (Holtham, 1996) which is stressed in Bent's definition. However, the tools used to manage information are frequently considered by management to be more important.

There is likewise an emphasis on information in organisations, and in particular in for-profit organisations, where information management and information technology management are considered to be one and the same. **Information resources management (IRM)** refers to the identification, assessment and use of information resources, once again specifically within organisations – and it is easy to see why this is often confused with IM.

> Information resources management is an umbrella term that covers the full range of management activities necessary to ensure that information is available in order to conduct business and to make decisions. IRM includes all types of data, numbers, text, images and

voice, made available using many different information and communications technologies. An infrastructural 'platform' is used to acquire, store, process, distribute and retrieve the data. (Beaumont and Sutherland, 1992: 16)

Strategic planning is about being able to respond to change. The Strategic Information Institute identifies *strategic information management (SIM)* as 'the body of knowledge created by the emergence of the Internet and other technologies and the proliferation of mergers and business alliances'. This does not give a clear idea of what this 'body of knowledge' comprises. However, SIM usually involves the use of information for strategic advantage.

An essential issue with these dimensions of information management and the TIPs is that 'management' is not a term easily appropriated by the liberal-humanist trained professionals who dominate the TIPs. At the same time, the management of information in human enterprise is critical.

Semantic confusion

The lack of practicable definitions of the concepts central to the IPs – data, information and knowledge – have led to much uncertainty, and this is compounded when 'documents', 'records', 'communication' and 'information resources' are considered. The most frequent explanation of these abstract notions involves a hierarchy: that data are the basic ingredients of information; that information is a selection of data; and knowledge is processed or absorbed information. The differences between the concepts are not fully characterised. As I have noted elsewhere (Myburgh, 2000), a different way of regarding the relationship between data, information and knowledge clarifies the relationship between them and hints at how they might be managed.

Such semantic clarification adopts a pragmatic approach. While the terms are often used interchangeably, most would argue that there are in fact differences in meaning and it would follow that there are differences in application. Each notion can therefore be interpreted in order to formulate its practical consequences, as what is understood by these terms will determine certain actions and practices. If there are no practical differences, then all of these terms would mean the same thing (James, 1907). Should there be differences between information, data and knowledge, it would follow that there would be concomitant differences between information, data and knowledge management.

Knowledge

Rather than considering data as the basic unit of information and knowledge, understanding knowledge itself is considered primary. This is a complex concept, but a clear understanding is vital.

Consider this statement by Rowley: 'Librarians can become knowledge professionals in three dimensions: managing knowledge repositories, facilitating knowledge flow and communication, and leveraging value generation capacity' (Rowley, 2003). She touches here on characteristics of information, documents and communication and how knowledge is created and valued – and, as a result, there is no a clear idea of what is actually being discussed.

'Knowledge' is an abstract noun, a result of the verb 'to know' and is therefore something possessed by people, and does not exist separately.

> *Knowledge*: 1. the facts or experiences known by a person or group of people. 2. the state of knowing. 3. consciousness or familiarity gained by experience or learning. 4. erudition or informed learning. 5. specific information about a subject. (*Collins' Dictionary*)

Peter Drucker concurs:

> Knowledge does not reside in a book, a databank, a software program; they contain only information [or data]. Knowledge is always embodied in a person; carried out by a person; created, augmented, and improved by a person; applied by a person; taught and passed on by a person; used or misused by a person. (Drucker, 1993: 210)

Foskett's distinctions between data, information and knowledge form the basis of the approach taken here. His distinction rests to a large extent on a communication model rather than any artefact or technology. He declares:

> Knowledge is what I know.
> Information is what we know (i.e. shared knowledge). Communication is the imparting or interchange of information by speech, writing or signs, i.e. the transfer of knowledge.
> Data (literally *things given*) are any facts assumed to be a matter of direct observation. (Foskett, 1996)

It can be argued that knowledge exists before data. Knowledge has traditionally been separated by philosophers into knowledge by acquaintance (knowledge gained by experience) and knowledge by description (knowledge gained by reading and facts). Humans start gaining knowledge by experience from at least the moment of birth as input is provided through the five senses. As we are born with individual characteristics, capacities and personalities, we each have a different understanding of reality. Further knowledge is derived from others.

Therefore, it could be said that some knowledge is derived from data, some from information and some from how intellect and personality process these. Each individual, as a result, possesses a unique body of knowledge, as knowledge can be understood as the psychological result of perception, learning and reasoning.

There are some differences between the cognitive and constructionist views of knowledge. The cognitivist view holds that learning comprises information processing and is a linear process, subsequent upon the identification and acquisition of suitable information. In this way, uncertainty is reduced and 'truth' is discovered. Knowledge, in this view, is a universal, explicit object which represents reality and truth, and relies only upon successful communication to be disseminated.

The constructionist view, on the other hand, views knowledge as personal and individual, relying on an individual context, experience and interpretation. Learning depends on the sense made of it, which relies on languages of various kinds, and therefore depends on individual socialisation. Any knowledge that is 'true' relies, for this characteristic, on what has been legitimised by society.

Knowledge as a concept has yet more complexity. Nonaka and Takeuchi (1995) explain *explicit knowledge* as that knowledge which can be expressed in language in a manner understandable to another person, and which can be captured and codified. *Tacit knowledge* is an individual's unique compilation of experience and information, but also understanding or insight which may exist only in a preverbal form. It is therefore difficult (if not impossible) to communicate knowledge.

Tacit knowledge can therefore be considered as 'knowledge', as defined above, while explicit knowledge is more like 'information', that part of knowledge that can be communicated. This has led Wilson to write a most interesting article on KM, in which he declares that it sounds just like information management (Wilson, 2002), begging the question whether separation between the two is really possible.

Tenkasi and Boland (1998) differentiate further between the following types of knowledge:

- *privileged knowledge* – scientific, rational knowledge enjoys a privileged social status within western culture – and funding;

- *cultural knowledge* – explicit, tacit, encoded and embedded or the collective form of knowledge expressed in routines, norms and cultural traditions;

- *rational and professional knowledge* – formal, rational and elitist, with a distinction between knowledge acquired formally and knowledge acquired on the job (Tenkasi and Boland, 1998).

Knowledge, therefore, in spite of the complexities which may arise for researchers in philosophy, education or KM, can practicably be stated to be that which people know and is accumulated through understanding, interpreting, analysing and making meaning of what is experienced and observed, as well as what others have communicated.

Information

In spite of frenzied use of the term 'information' in a variety of contexts, it is not always clear what is meant by it – or rather, it seems to mean what the user wants it to mean, rather like Humpty Dumpty in *Alice in Wonderland*: 'When

I say a word it means exactly what I want it to mean, no more and no less' (Dodgson, 1865).

'Information' is arguably an even more difficult concept to define than 'knowledge' as it appears in so many guises, leading to the dizzy heights of philosophy.[1] Bateson defines information as 'a difference that makes a difference' (Bateson, 1980: 17), while 'knowledge is a difference that makes a difference that makes a difference' (Bateson, 1973). Elsewhere he regards information simply as the 'reduction in uncertainty' (Bateson, 1980).

As indicated by Foskett (1996), information is that part of knowledge which can be shared or communicated, although not solely by language: it might take the form of a colour, a picture or the dance that bees do when they discover a flowerbed. Information constitutes messages which can be understood and make sense, thereby reducing uncertainty. Information, unlike knowledge, exists independently of the medium on which it is recorded or the technology which makes it available (whereas knowledge can only exist in a person's head), as information can be communicated without being recorded, such as in a conversation or a performance. There is, however, often some confusion between information and the physical artefact on which it might be recorded: information is not a document. Another common confusion is between data and information, which is found in some disciplines (such as computer science) and even in some dictionary definitions.

In its reified expression (as some kind of physical 'thing') information has come to be regarded as an economic pillar or resource, described by Best (1996) as the 'fourth resource' after money, labour and plant. It is viewed as something which can be capitalised, which has a fundamental value and to which cost accounting techniques can be applied. Information is considered to have specific characteristics, uses and a life cycle, and something that can be transformed into useful (or valuable) outputs (Ellis, 1996). This is not dissimilar to the librarians' understanding that reading makes people 'better'.

In spite of this, there continues to be a general ignorance of the value and importance of information within organisations. There is a lack of awareness that decisions are sometimes based on insufficient or inaccurate information, that poorly arranged information can result in considerable staff and storage costs. Information can also get lost in storage technologies if not properly organised. Information is expensive to create, acquire, arrange and store, and because these costs are difficult to determine, they are frequently ignored.

Organisations are generally unaware of the cost of the information which they are producing. The creation or production, acquisition, arrangement and storage of information (not to mention unnecessary duplication) costs more than IT. One major reason for this ignorance is the difficulty of putting a monetary value on the former tasks, whereas it is easy to read a financial statement detailing the costs of hardware and software.

There is an ongoing public conviction that 'information' means IT, as previously noted, and that information problems can be solved with IT. However, as Robert Solow famously stated in 1987, 'You can see the Computer Age everywhere except in the productivity statistics.' This is known as the 'productivity paradox', and indicates that it is information, rather than IT, that is more important.

Information is that part of an individual's knowledge which can be communicated, which has meaning and which can be understood by another individual. It can often, but not always, be represented in various forms (language, dance, colour, shape) or recorded on various media (paper, film, stone, silicon chips). Only part of a person's knowledge can be communicated as information.

> Knowledge that can be turned into words or pictures can be 'objectified' in various ways for communication purposes. Some part of knowledge, however, must be left behind in the body that gathered it, felt it, stored it, and massaged it. Only abstractions (print, ideographs) and models can be objectified and made into machine-readable representations. Indeed, 'representations' is just the word to use. Knowledge representations are not knowledge but rather representations of knowledge. (Budd, 1999: 34)

As Ingwersen (1992) points out, the concept of information must include the processes by which the informant's knowledge is transformed by the act of communication and the processes of perception, evaluation, interpretation and learning, in which the information seeker's knowledge is transformed.

Agre (1995) makes the point that '... information is an element of certain professional ideologies, most particularly librarianship and computing, and cannot be understood except through the practices within which it is constructed by the members of those professions in their work'. He argues that we need to understand and question the ideologies which give rise to particular understandings of the concept of information, which are not absolute but relative. It is only in this way, he maintains, that information management will be able to justify its social relevance in contemporary society.

Data

Data is the plural for *datum*, a given, a single element that is factual and quantifiable. Many data are measurements and are frequently expressed in numbers. They are generally simple in their attributes and possess only one unambiguous property.

Data in their pure form can be received, stored, processed and transmitted by humans or computers. Data do not have an intrinsic discrete meaning, but they can easily be assessed in terms of accuracy. The sales figures for a certain month, the height of a building or the colour of a flower can all be expressed as data. It is rare that a fact on its own, e.g. '42', will have much meaning, except where it contextually appears as an answer to a question (such as, famously, 'What is the meaning of life?'[2]).

Data are created through observation and measurement of the natural phenomena that surround us, in an attempt to understand the nature of reality. Established measuring instruments and systems are used to measure temperature, height, distance, quantity, intensity and so forth. Accuracy of measurement is important for interpretation and for outcome, and flawed measuring systems can result in faulty data. Variations in measurement can lead to a different understanding of the nature of reality.[3]

However, data by themselves do not tell us much. Knowing how many pairs of red shoes were sold during April tells us only that: 128 pairs of red shoes were sold in April. What is more useful is understanding why they were sold: is there a cult fashion for red shoes? Are there many people like Dorothy who wish to escape Oz and return to Kansas?[4] Answering questions like these can indicate further demand for red shoes.

These measurements, or data, must then be kept unpolluted and in proper relationship to one another. There should be a consecutive and sequential relationship between data sets to allow useful analysis.

Metadata

'Metadata' as a term has really only gained currency since the advent of the World Wide Web (WWW), around 1995. It is, however, a functional class of data that has been around since the *Pinakes* of Callimachus[5] (even though he was inclined to provide full information about the works held by the Alexandrian Library). A simple definition is that metadata is used to describe other data or information, like a library catalogue entry.

Metadata can be used to describe objects, documents or abstract concepts, which are called 'entities', in terms of their most important attributes, for example author, telephone number, height and so forth. In the case of describing documents, metadata can be used to describe the physical (even if virtual) characteristics of a document, as well the intellectual content – what the document is about. Classification schemes and indexing schemas both provide metadata. Metadata are used by IPs to control (and arrange) documents and to facilitate the retrieval of both documents and information: a metadata record thus acts as a surrogate for the larger complete document.

The matter of deciding how to describe a document or piece of information in a database is not an easy one. It is not simply a matter of reading off self-evident properties of items, but a highly skilled interpretative activity 'by which the properties of items are not only described, but stabilised and even created' (Levy, 1995). While some rules and activities might change when it comes to the management of certain types of entities such as records, the basic purpose and function remain the same.

Work on metadata has, to a certain extent, been re-invented by information systems developers. In computers, the term 'metadata' is used specifically to refer to data that are instrumental in transforming raw data into processed data. For instance, it is metadata such as a field definition that indicates a given stream of bits is a customer's address, part of a photographic image or a code fragment in a given computer's machine language.

Communication

Communication is the process of exchanging information via a common system of symbols and can take various forms. It might be transitory, such as a dance, poetry recital or song; information may also be recorded or captured via some technology, such as paper or film, which allows the information to be released from spatio-temporal limitations. Some kinds of knowledge cannot be easily communicated, as they rely on less common forms of communication such as poetry, dance, music or art; yet other types of knowledge can only be suggested symbolically or grasped intuitively, such as religious faith, the appreciation of beauty or creative activity.

The standard communication model so often cited, even in communications studies, is that of engineers Shannon and Weaver (Shannon, 1948; Weaver and Shannon, 1949) and, is little more than a transmission model drawn from engineering which suits the clear 'communication' of simple entities such as data. It is clear that according to this model, the emphasis is on access rather than understanding. It does not lend itself usefully to the communication of information which depends, *inter alia*, on the language, culture, knowledge infrastructure and context of both the user and the receiver for correct 'transmission'.

Words themselves have no fixed meaning, and successful communication depends on the contexts and codes or languages of the receiver and sender coinciding. In addition to understanding, Capurro adds that:

> A message we send or receive is to be called information if, and only if, it entails the possibility of changing in a significant manner something of our previous ways of relating to ourselves, to other persons, to things and to situations in the world. (Capurro, 1996)

Understanding and using information is reliant on a variety of contextual variables, including the various social, economic, technical and political contexts of the individual, time, language and existing individual knowledge. Much of the understanding of context is derived from communication studies, which can also help us understand how people make sense, meaning and use of information (e.g. Dervin, 1977). Gerbner declares that 'The concept of information, divorced from social and cultural contexts and functions, is misleading and potentially mischievous' (Gerbner, 1988).

The double notions of information as both facts and communication are inherent in the foundations of information theory, in particular cybernetics as developed by Norbert Weiner in 1948. Wiener based much of his work on systems theory and introduced engineering concepts such as entropy, feedback and noise as characteristics of how the human brain interprets and makes meaning of information.

The aspect of communication also clarifies essential distinctions between data, information and knowledge. Data can be transmitted and recorded, but not really communicated as they do not rely on meaning or understanding; knowledge is created individually, but only part of it can be communicated, usually through iterative processes; information, however, is that which is communicated.

Information resources

It is important to distinguish between information and information resources as confusion of these concepts is widely found, not least in the area of information economics, where information resources are referred to more commonly than information itself. Information resources include the actual information, as well as the services, packages, documents, support technologies and systems used to generate, store, organise, move and display information. They include data, published and unpublished documents, experts, computer hardware and software, records and so on.

Documents

The term 'document' refers to any recording of information – information is contained in a document (not dissimilar to a glass jar which holds strawberry jam). A documentalist's notion of a document is as a generic term to denote any physical information resource. As Briet famously stated, even an antelope can be a document, as it contains, or represents, information in logical and dynamic dimensions (Briet, 1951). People themselves may be regarded as knowledge or information containers.

While all documents are containers of information, they are of different types, and different types of document are dealt with by different professional groups, in their manufacture and in their organisation and management. Documents can be differentiated by purpose (legal, ephemera), function (archival materials, comics, textbooks) or medium (digital, magnetic tape, paper).

Documents comprise different components, some of which are unique to documents of certain types, but most of which have equivalents in all documents. For example, few documents lack a creator, and they all come into existence on a specific date which can be measured.

Documents are like nodes in a network – they are often connected to each other by sharing authors, publishers, date of publication, citing similar documents, and referring to others. There can also be multiple versions – revisions, translations, editions and transitions into different media.

Records

Some documents are records. Records are a special category and require distinctive treatment because of their unique qualities. They cannot be identified from the majority of documents by format, media, age or size: the principle of division that distinguishes them is that they provide evidence of business activity. The *Australian Standard* defines a record as

> recorded information, in any form, including data in computer systems, created or received and maintained by an organization or person in the transaction of business or the conduct of affairs and kept as evidence of such activity.

Records therefore are documents that detail the activities, transactions, policies and procedures of an organisation, and have both financial and legal values. Records are subject to similar rules of creation, format, media, communication and even description and identification as other documents, but they have an additional value: they provide evidence of how things were done and by whom. This is sometimes referred to as (corporate) 'memory', and this distinction is made by an archivist.

Information systems

It is probably of interest to note at this point that 'information systems' are understood as a system of entities, including people, processes and resources, which store, organise and disseminate information. Most frequently, even though an information system does not have to include IT, there is a strong correlation in practice; added to this, people are often excluded from the notion of information systems. Allen supports the idea that the term

> 'information system' does not refer simply to a technology or to a family of technologies, but includes humans in several different capacities. IT is only one fragment of an information system. (Allen, 1996: 6)

However, as information is seen as part of the process of communication, an information system can be defined as a linked and related set of items or entities that contribute to the process of becoming informed. An information system can exist without any technology at all, and possibly even without documents, as it is related to the exchange of information. A verbal grapevine is a form of information system.

Information systems were first identified as communication systems by Parker and Paisley (1966) which was a significant conceptual breakthrough and opened the door to more sociological and cultural approaches to the evaluation of such systems. Studying information systems as a type of communication system embedded in a social and organisational discourse can take into account the unique hybridity of technology and culture that ICTs represent.

This position allows consideration of a number of contextual issues which assist in making meaning of information, as noted previously. An inclusive view of an information system situates users and their information needs as important components of a system, and indicates the necessity to understand the coding and representation of knowledge, the mechanics of IT and the information need being resolved.

It should be noted that many information systems are in fact metadata systems, and used for document, rather than information, retrieval.

Data retrieval systems

A data retrieval system stores and retrieves data. Often such a system is referred to as an information retrieval system, particularly when data can be 'massaged' or processed in some way by the system, although the result still comprises data. Techniques of data retrieval are closely allied to the nature of data (simple, not complex) and its way of being entered into or captured by a system. Because of the nature of data, data retrieval is usually fairly unambiguous. Data can be entered into a system, be retrieved in their immaculate state, and yet still contain the same meaning.

Document retrieval systems

A document is a container for information and data. As noted, many information retrieval systems are actually document retrieval systems, although generally it is the actual information in the document that is required rather than the metadata of the document surrogate. The library catalogue is an example of a document retrieval system.

Text retrieval

A text retrieval system searches through blocks of words or language looking for term matches and is concerned with word or phrase frequency. Text processing methods have evolved to handle the problem of matching terms with search requests without formal indexing languages with which end-users might not be familiar. Words are considered as data and an adequate representation of the content of the document.

Information retrieval systems

An information retrieval (IR) system is a type of information system which is able to identify documents (or text) which contain the desired information and suppress the recall of irrelevant information. Often an information retrieval system is actually a data or document retrieval system which retrieves metadata. The Internet is an example of an information retrieval system which is able to provide the information itself rather than just a reference to it.

Components of an automated IR system include a database structure which includes logical and physical structures, metadata describing the entities (or documents), query languages (frequently Boolean based), sometimes natural language searching, and sorting mechanisms such as similarity and association measures and weighting.

Evaluation of data, information and knowledge

The three concepts – knowledge, data and information – vary in how they are created, organised, recorded, disseminated, communicated, evaluated, sought for and used. It is particularly in the techniques for evaluation of data, information and knowledge that the distinctions between the terms become clear.

Evaluation of data

Data is evaluated in terms of accuracy, validity, completeness, relevance, timeliness, auditability and integrity. Data must meet these criteria at the time of inclusion into a system, and retain an immaculate and unpolluted state until retrieved. Davis notes that:

> The legal concept of a chain of evidence is a good way to visualise data integrity. Unless you can prove that no one tampered with the evidence between the time it was collected and the time it is presented in court, that evidence is inadmissible. Similarly, unless you can prove that specific data came from an approved source and that only sanctioned changes were made since they were collected, those data cannot be trusted. (Davis, 1995: 136)

Evaluating documents

Traditional IPs usually evaluate documents using the criteria of format, scope of content, relation to other works, authority of author and publisher, treatment, arrangement, cost and longevity. In this way, an attempt is made to estimate the value of the information that the document contains, although a close examination of how and why the information was produced is generally not undertaken.

Evaluating records

Records are assessed by the criteria of authenticity, completeness and accuracy, and whether they are understandable, meaningful and comprehensive. Record-keepers typically pay scant attention to the information which is contained in records, which may have great strategic or competitive value, in addition to evidential value.

Evaluating information

Information can be evaluated in terms of authority, currency and completeness, but the real value of information is relative rather than absolute: it has value to an individual or organisation usually only at a specific time and place. This fickle, suggestive nature of the value of information creates great difficulties for information professionals who wish to convince senior management of their usefulness. Equally intangible is the unpredictability of forecasting what information might, in the future, become important.

The value of information can also be influenced by the context of use, which can affect the processes of making meaning and sense out of information. 'Context' can include the language abilities, previous knowledge and intelligence of a user: in fact, all cognitive and affective characteristics. The notion of 'relevance' is closely tied to the evaluation of information, and this remains a difficult and unresolved term.

Evaluating knowledge

Knowledge is often associated with 'truth' as exploring knowledge, what it is and how it is constructed usually takes place through the processes of philosophy. However, it is the objective of most disciplines to create knowledge (in the process of discovering 'truth'), and this outcome is determined by disciplinary outlooks such as which problems are to be studied and how they will be studied. Understanding how research is done in various disciplines assists in interpreting the validity of the information recorded; it also serves to indicate the type of knowledge or knowledge framework that is likely to be encountered in a discipline.

How these definitions may work

On a general and disciplinary level, there is a considerable lack of conceptual clarity between the essential terms 'data', 'information', 'knowledge' and 'documents', as well as the different types of systems that are used to manage and control them. This does not bode well for the identification of a common theoretical basis for the IPs, in particular as there are often considerable discrepancies in outlook and objectives among the various groups who work in different areas of the field. Concentrating on the TIPs, it is now time to consider the paradigm, or mould, which frames and guides the discipline of information management.

Notes

1. See, for example, Capurro (1996) 'On the genealogy of information', and (2002) 'The concept of information'; see also Hjørland (2000b).
2. According to Douglas Adams (2002) in his cult book, *Life, the Universe and Everything,* part of the *Hitchhiker's Guide to the Galaxy* series – 'A Trilogy in Five Parts'.
3. A report on 11 January 2002 indicated that, after examining 200,000 galaxies, Ivan K. Baldry and Karl Glazebrook from Johns Hopkins University in Baltimore, Maryland, determined that the average colour of the universe was pale turquoise. On 8 March 2002, they changed this to beige, apparently because the

computers had been incorrectly set (available online at: *http:// news.bbc.co.uk/1/hi/sci/tech/1861957.stm*).

4. Baum (1993).

5. Callimachus was an important librarian, bio-bibliographer and cataloguer at the Alexandrian Library in the 3rd century BC, and is sometimes referred to as the 'Founding Father' of librarians. His work known as the *Pinakes* was an early chrono-logical subject catalogue containing information about the texts, their authors and authenticity (Brittany, 2000).

3

The TIP paradigm and habitus

Public perception of the TIPs

The traditional information professions share a number of characteristics, such as managing a range of documents and other artefacts that contain information. However, they also share a stereotypical negative image, which has been discussed over some time in the literature, without, however, an examination of why this negative image still prevails.

The public perception of librarians is that they are people in charge of books housed in a building called a library; records managers are perceived as filing clerks, and archivists as individuals dealing with anything old and dusty. The reason for this state of affairs is the poorly understood nature of information work. Most people (including senior management) don't know what traditional information professionals do or can do: they are largely invisible. Not only do the general public not know what traditional IPs do, but few traditional IPs themselves are clear on this point. They have thus far been unsuccessful in persuading others of their value to contemporary society and are unprepared for the competition which they have encountered. As a consequence, these professions enjoy little authority and are often considered unnecessary.

There are a number of apocryphal myths surrounding the nature of information work which, in general, serve to confuse rather than clarify, enhancing the negative stereotype. For example, there is a belief that the traditional IPs provide for those who like to read; there is a close link between admirers of English (in particular) literature, and those who wish to become librarians. There is a fancy that IPs spend most of their working life selecting 'good' books in order to function as cultural leaders in their communities. The reality is that information professionals do everything (well, nearly) to documents except read them. Further, the content, context and medium of the documents with which IPs deal vary from sculptures to Post-It™ notes. Many may never see a 'book'.

Information work is considered to be suitable for shy, self-effacing people who work quietly among sacred cultural relics and avoid confronting situations. The reality is that, as with most cultural institutions such as hairdressers and pubs, libraries and information centres are public spaces, which means that people not only can, but do, come into them. Admittedly, this 'public' is sometimes a defined one, but anything can happen with people, and probably will. And the whole point of information work is supposedly to get out there to assist people in satisfying their information needs ...

The nature of information work is understood to comprise organising containers of information: the traditional IP waits for users to ask for something and then helps them find it. Such a passive approach extends to using complicated and arcane systems for organising information materials. In the next breath, of course, because of the commonly understood model of information literacy, users are expected to pick up enough knowledge of such systems in a one-hour induction course to know not to bother the traditional IP again.

In reality, many traditional IPs have a rather incomplete knowledge of cataloguing, classification and indexing, although they generally grow accustomed to the system that they work with. They have little sense of the abstraction of these principles, and get flummoxed when others talk about epistemologies, taxonomies and ontologies, even though these are at the heart of the work of TIPs.

Another reason why individuals are attracted to these professions is that they are seen as a pathway to a steady, lifelong job. Research has indicated that many graduates never get jobs in libraries or formal information centres (e.g. Brittain, 1995;[1] KALIPER, 2000) and that the usual education offered to the TIPs does not provide the skills and competencies that organisations need (Myburgh and Nimon, 2001).

This leads us to the next myth, which is that the library or information centre is a place and space where traditional IPs practice their profession, usually on physical items (or digital replicas of physical items). This gives rise to an inordinate fear of IT, which subversively makes the store of documents vanish. It is impossible to duplicate the information centre in cyberspace (at least, this is not done by TIPs). By believing this myth, there is lack of recognition that information-seeking behaviour happens everywhere, constantly. If people feel that they need to know something, the repository of documents is often the place of very last resort – and sometimes not even worth the effort, as doing without the information entirely is often seen as preferable (according to Zipf's law of least effort) (Zipf, 1949).

Added to this fear, ICTs are seen as the uncompromising enemies and destroyers of documents, the TIPs as professions, and information places as social institutions. In the case of librarians there are many who fear that ICT will spell the end of reading. The practice of reading is very strongly associated with warehouses of documents, particularly in libraries that do not lend their materials. Reading is, quite rightly, viewed as a beneficial activity for a number of reasons. However, it seems reasonably clear that paper will not vanish, and that libraries, archives and records centres will not die. Nonetheless, if modern lifestyles are such that many are too busy to read, or have gained new literacies or sources of entertainment, document centres might well need to respond in more innovative ways to demonstrate their value, by reassessing and redefining their social role.

For practitioners, professional associations are highly regarded, prominent in maintaining standards, providing political clout and leading the professions forward. However, as associations are, redundantly speaking, comprised of members, and many associations consist almost exclusively of TIP practitioners employed by large libraries (notably public and academic), this becomes a self-fulfilling prophecy.

The cutting edge of the profession is substantially ignored, as the many practitioners in new information jobs simply do not belong to such organisations. IFLA (2000) has stated that traditional programmes 'have focused on developing physical collections of books and other materials in library buildings staffed by people who have learned to select, acquire, organise, retrieve and circulate these materials ... [but] today the emphasis is on the individual practitioner and the concentration is on information provision in a variety of contexts'.

The professional association could guide the profession. Instead, we are faced with an abundance of professional associations to meet the needs of various areas: the American Library Association, the Association of Knowledgework, the Records Management Society of Great Britain, the Association of Records Managers and Administrators International, the Society of American Archivists, the International Congress of Archivists, the Society of Competitive Intelligence Professionals, the Australian Library and Information Association, the Association for Information Science and Technology, the Association of Image and Information Management, the Knowledge and Information Society – and many others. And for the most part they don't talk to each other, with few exceptions, such as the Alliance of Libraries, Archives and Records Managers (ALARM), in Canada.[2]

Another myth firmly adhered to by practitioners and their employers alike is that, miraculously, information workers are able to offer specialised services to huge communities of people in mass mode, delivering the same kind of care and individual attention that specialist medical professionals offer on a one-to-one basis, with a supporting cast of other professionals and para-professionals, specialised locations and equipment. In reality, information users are left to their own devices. It is like going to a hospital, being shown your bed and how to diagnose your complaint, how to perform your own appendectomy, and subsequently how to convalesce in an appropriate manner – with the professional looking in on you from time to time.

While some of these myths have been slightly exaggerated, they are not entirely risible. A myth has great power in constructing a particular ethos, or even a mindset. A person, profession or organisation can be imbued with attributes which may exist only in the imagination but are believed to be true, and the myth provides some meaning and structure for such beliefs. As Eward Said explained: 'There are no innocent, no unideological myths, just as there are not 'natural' myths. Every myth is a manufactured object, and it is the inherent bad faith of a myth to seem, or rather to pretend, to be a fact' (Said, 1986: 83).

These myths serve two purposes: they contribute to the formation of the image of the profession and satisfy a public perception of the validity of the institutions; they also serve to authorise mythical activities of the TIPs. An entire body of myths, a mythology, might be associated with an institution or professional culture. Barthes has examined the tendency of contemporary social value systems to create modern myths, which he explores in some detail in *Mythologies* (Barthes, 1972), which interestingly contributed substantially to the development of cultural studies.

In his analysis, myths in turn create simplified models or archetypes, which become a metonymic code which represents the TIPs. Thus we have the archetypal librarian who works in a library and stamps books; this librarian is a middle-aged spinster with spectacles and a bun (how can this image ever fade?) who is in a position of power and control, but only in her domain. Jung held that archetypes are innate prototypes for ideas, and while many may dismiss or even become outraged at the persistence of this archetype, it is deeply involved with the interpretation of the profession as it is observed and experienced.

These myths must be dispelled, but not only on a superficial level, such as changing the terminology used or isolating various areas of the discipline (such as information science), which serves to confound the issue further. Traditional IPs must move out of their comfort zone and change their mindset, which is the most dangerous threat to the traditional information professions as it results in an inability to respond fully to a changing environment.

What is a TIP paradigm?

A paradigm is the prevailing and generally accepted perspective of a particular discipline at a particular time and it is used as a model or pattern for the practices of the discipline. The notion of a paradigm originated with Kuhn (1962), who defined a paradigm as ' ... the set of symbolic generalisations, shared commitment to beliefs in models, exemplars, tacit knowledge and intuition' in any given community of specialists (Kuhn, 1970: 182–98). He specifically examined the creation of knowledge in science, where he believes research activity is characterised by paradigms. These 'disciplinary matrices' provide scientists with scientific norms and values, orientations toward phenomena, rules to identify which problems are important and which trivial, and methodological examples upon which to model efforts of enquiry.

What are the 'symbolic generalisations' and beliefs that IPs share? The TIP paradigm can be divided into two areas: theory and praxis.

Paradigm of TIP praxis

In 1887, Melville Dewey established the School of Library Economy at Columbia University, New York, and in so doing established a paradigm of applied skills. Dewey was a firm believer in practical instruction, and his views have informed library education up to the present. This approach has meant there has been traditionally little emphasis on theory in professional education for librarians, archivists or records managers – all the traditional document management professions.

Pierce Butler noted in 1933, '... the librarian is strangely uninterested in the theoretical aspects of his profession ... The librarian ... stands alone in the simplicity of his pragmatism: a rationalization of each immediate technical process by itself seems to satisfy his intellectual interest' (Butler, 1933: 26). There is a continuing emphasis in professional education on gaining practical skills. This is probably the most distinguishing feature of differences between the IPs, while paradoxically being the point of most convergence.

Because of the clear split between theory and practice, there is a concomitant tension between academics and practitioners regarding the balance between the two, and, so far, it appears that the appeasing of practitioners by academics remains an important consideration because of the associated necessary accreditation by a professional association. This has also contributed to the lack of theoretical education or development. Hjørland notes that:

> It is common in schools of library and information science to give practical instruction in the use of information sources and information technology. This does not indicate that these colleges see themselves as theoretically oriented. Even less they see themselves as being researchers and part of a 'science'. (Hjørland, 2000a)

This is largely true in archival studies and records management as well. Saracevic observes that the pervasive technical nature of the curriculum in the absence of a strong theoretical base 'easily deteriorates into vocational rather than professional education' (Saracevic, 1994: 195), which has resulted in a blurring between professional and paraprofessional work.

Added to this is the notion of habitus: a habitus can construct a paradigm. While habitus is defined by Bourdieu as the total ideational environment of a person, the term can also indicate the limitations of practitioners who are trained in a certain set of beliefs concerning a discipline or profession. Habitus is defined by Van House as:

> ... a system of dispositions determined by past experience, particularly by one's class, education, and profession. Habitus functions as a matrix of perceptions, appreciations, and actions. Habitus is the means by which a field perpetuates itself through the voluntary

actions of its members. It gives the appearance of rationality and intentionality to behaviour that is less than fully conscious. How individuals interpret a situation and the actions that they consider possible are unconsciously constrained by their habitus. Action guided by habitus has the appearance of rationality but is based not so much on reason as on socially-constituted dispositions. (Van House, 1996)

The concept of habitus brings attention to the fact that there are limitless options for action, but these are not all considered due to social, cultural or professional conditioning. A person or profession's actions are guided by the view of the world that is held, and it is not normally consciously realised that different views or courses of action even exist. Working within the context of a particular discipline can constrain and affect the way in which problems are seen and tackled; the content determines the kinds of perspectives which emerge from the study of the discipline. Becher (1989) found that this influence can be so pervasive as to shape social structures within disciplines and the political and social relationships between disciplines.

The TIP paradigm of praxis contains the following elements:

- TIP practice is focused on place, specifically warehouses of documents, although each of these 'warehouses' originates in response to a specific community's information needs and to this extent they differ. There is emphasis on the building itself for serving community interests (including chess competitions and art shows). Van House urges TIPs to 'decouple' themselves from libraries (and, by extension, other warehouses of documents), arguing that much discussion revolves around the institution rather than 'an abstraction of [the TIP] knowledge base' (Van House, 1996).

■ These institutions are staffed by people who have learned to select, acquire, organise, retrieve and circulate documents rather than the information contained in the documents. This focus on the management of documents is understood by practitioners and the public alike. As Budd reports:

> Much of the discourse on knowledge within the discipline of LIS does not consider the epistemic nature and purposes of knowledge. Rather, there seems to be a tacit acceptance of Karl Popper's notion of objective knowledge, particularly his subdivision of knowledge he refers to as World 3. This third world consists of the record of knowledge, including books and libraries. (Budd, 1998)

■ TIPs typically select, from the universe of available documents, those which are believed to be appropriate matches for the information demands of a particular clientele. There is little investigation into how or why, or the manner in which, the information in these documents has been created, and there are few tests of its value or validity. Most assessment is done at face value: author, publisher, date and the like. Interpretation of statistics, demography, geographic information and expert information, for example, fall beyond their scope. There is usually no close examination of the information needs of the clientele, or how they would search for useful information.

■ Success in the role of document management comprises the delivery of documents or bibliographic references deemed to be an appropriate response to an information request. There is little formal follow-up, such as assessing whether the information was meaningful or useful, or indeed how it might have been used to assist decision-making or learning outcomes.

- Much of what is seen as 'core' TIP work is determining the organisation of documents in relation to one another. The central assumption of the TIP tradition is that information exists independently of human action and has its own natural order and organisation.

- A major professional achievement is the application of various standardised metadata codes. In librarianship, these are the Anglo-American Cataloguing Rules Version 2 (AACR2 (Revised)), the Dewey Decimal Classification System (DDC) and the Library of Congress Subject Headings (LCSH) (even though much research suggests that interpretation of these internationally recognised codes is irregular and subjective, but that can be discussed later). This could be called the 'Procrustean bed of linear arrangement', as it has little to do with the nature or structure of knowledge but rather with how to arrange artefacts in a meaningful order. Traditional IPs are seldom required to develop, modify or critique such codes, which are peculiar to certain cultures and times, and usually hegemonic. As Radford notes:

> In the Western literary tradition, the library has long been taken as a metaphor for order and rationality. It represents, in institutional form, the ultimate realization of a place where each item within it has a fixed place and stands in an *a priori* relationship with every other item. The rationality of the library in many ways represents the description of nature idealized by the institution of positivist science ... Indexes, catalogs and other information retrieval systems act as road

maps to navigate this environment of knowledge. (Radford, 1998)

- Traditional IPs are viewed as maintainers of order and discipline. The traditional IP seeks to exercise rationality and control over the collection of documents and the user is too often seen as a chaotic aberration in the divine order of things.

- When users are not being seen as invaders in an orderly universe, they are constructed in a deficiency model, being ignorant, useless and needy – and generalised. This is the so-called user-centred approach, and is found embodied in outreach and information literacy programmes. In this capacity, the role of the traditional IP is as access and location provider, and interpreter of systems. Little attention is paid to the user per se, but only to the user vis-à-vis the information system.

- The user is understood only as someone for whom access to documents is necessary. The user's motivation for accessing such documents is not fully examined, nor are the results of such access.

- There is lack of clarity concerning the actual cultural or societal niche of the TIPs: it is hard to understand the rules of the game when it is not clear what game is being played.

Paradigm of TIP theory

'Theory' can be defined as 'the coherent set of hypothetical, conceptual, and pragmatic principles forming the general frame of reference for a field of inquiry (as for deducing principles, formulating hypotheses, undertaking action)'. A theoretical frame of reference should provide an understanding of the societal role of the professions and suggest the processes and tasks that best support this role, and provide meaning to such actions and embodiments. Skills and competencies of practitioners normally follow from a theoretical understanding of the discipline.

'Where are the dead Germans?' asked Pierce, in a paper which deplored the lack of 'a common body of theory shaping the intellectual traditions of the field' (Pierce, 1992). McKechnie, Pettigrew and Joyce observe that 'past studies overwhelmingly suggest that the majority of LIS research is atheoretical' (McKechnie, Pettigrew and Joyce, 2001: 48).[3] This lack of theory in LIS presents what Foucault (Sheridan, 1980: 108) calls a 'low epistemological profile' – research in the TIPs is not very well developed in comparison with many other fields.

Having said this, there are writers in the IPs who have considered the field from a theoretical or philosophical point of view to establish conceptual foundations, notably Shera and Ranganathan (Brown-Syed, 1998). Contemporary writers in the theoretical and philosophical domain include Frohmann, Hjørland, Cornelius, Capurro, Floriadi and Day. Pierce argues that, for the most part, the classic theoretical and philosophical writers are ignored in education for LIS (Pierce, 1992). Saracevic (1994) notes that, typically, all that has been done is the addition of a few theoretical classes here and there to a required core, but a true theory of the IPs has not yet been defined, nor made available to students.

There is no fully articulated theoretical basis for the professional tasks that librarians either perform or control in the workplace, according to Danner (Danner, 1998), and this is true in records management and archives as well. Ostler and Dahlin emphasise the need for the profession to 'critically examine theories from all library thinkers and focus new energy on theory-building as an important professional responsibility' (1995).

The power of expertise relies on the boundedness, 'context, structuring and organization of knowledge provided in the narrow domains ... Knowledge can also be divided into theoretical knowledge and practical knowledge. Practical knowledge is essential for high performance, theoretical knowledge is essential for expert understanding, progress in the discipline, and adaptability – the ability to solve difficult and unique cases. Finally, knowledge can be viewed from the maturity of the domain – the degree of structure in the knowledge. Structured knowledge exists in well-understood domains; unstructured knowledge occurs when little is known in the field and there is no underlying theoretical framework. (Ostler, Dahlin and Willardson, 1995)

Kuhn notes that while 'the acquisition of a paradigm marks the sign of maturity in the development of any given scientific field' (Kuhn, 1970: 11) (as Ostler and Dahlin (1995) noted), research might nonetheless continue even without paradigms, but such knowledge is not structured. However, a paradigm is supposed to recognise theoretical consensus in a discipline: without a paradigm, perhaps there is no theoretical consensus.

Research is certainly done in the discipline, and includes case studies, performance measurements (which can include user questionnaires or circulation figures), information literacy, and user and non-user behaviour. Other areas of research include preservation, new electronic media and delivery, web use, education for the profession and investigations into the role of specific types of library, such as school libraries. Often this research is institution- or system-specific. Recently, there has been increasing interest in understanding the context of information-seeking behaviour, and exploration of the relationship between the user and ICTs.

A wide range of research methodologies has been used, including quantitative, qualitative, comparative, historical and, most recently, evidence-based librarianship. In some areas, such as informatics, bibliometrics and information retrieval, there have been conscious efforts to adopt scientific quantitative research methodologies, with varied success. Due in part to the ubiquitous and unique nature of information and the enormous range of potential research topics, as well as the clear distinction made between academics and practitioners, it is hardly surprising that no clear theoretical consensus can be identified within this paradigm. Frohmann disagrees, although in a qualified way, suggesting that the consensus as it exists is rather narrow.

> The literature of LIS reveals, in spite of the fuzziness of the discipline's institutional borders, a sufficiently clear set of discursive practices, grounded in its central institutional sites, which work together to construct specific interlocking identities for information, its users and its uses. The networks created by these identities, or subject positions, and their interrelationship configure the discursive resources available for the articulation of the field's problems. The ways in which its 'keywords' – 'information', 'information users' and 'information uses' – are used set the limits of possible questions, issues, hypotheses, demonstrations, data and research methodologies. (Frohmann, 1994)

In spite of a 'clear set of discursive practices', the limits set by these are negative due to the constrained and even confusing notions of 'information', 'information users' and 'information uses' which discourage disciplinary theory-building.

Several writers in the area, Jesse Shera and Herbert White among them, have noted the lack of a unified theoretical base which would identify the IPs, but there have been few attempts at identifying this. These writers foresaw that eventually this would be necessary (Shera, 1970; White, 1995) and it has become apparent that TIPs have not been entirely successful in even identifying the societal and organisational problems which are properly their task domain, or the other challenges which now face these professions. This has led to fragmentation, the development of new specialisations and encroachment by other groups (as nature abhors a vacuum).

Robbins-Carter and Seavey (1986) question whether there is indeed a theoretical base to library or information science or if the profession has borrowed from other disciplines like sociology or psychology. That the IPs have drawn on other disciplines is not a weakness, but in fact a necessity. The practice of the IPs needs to draw on (and contribute to) a variety of knowledges, and it is logical to assume that the theoretical base should likewise be multidisciplinary.

Creation of disciplinary knowledge

Knowledge is created as a result of attempts to understand reality, and this understanding develops through conception and perception. Ontology is a field of study that examines being and reality; Aristotle described ontology as 'the science of being *qua* being'. The work of ontology comprises determining what subjects and objects exist and what the relationship between them might be, what fundamental categories exist and what beings exist in such categories. Ontology is the theory of known reality rather than a theory of the process of knowing.

Closely related to ontology is epistemology, the branch of philosophy that deals, *inter alia*, with the nature, structure and origin of knowledge. Hamlyn defines epistemology as 'a branch of philosophy concerned with the nature and scope of knowledge, its presuppositions and basis, and the general reliability of claims to knowledge' (Hamlyn, 1967: 8–9) – in other words, it is the science of knowing, examining the nature of knowing and belief, how knowledge is possible. Epistemology also deals with a number of related problems: sense perception, the relations between the knower and the object known, the possible kinds of knowledge and the degrees of certainty for each kind of knowledge, the nature of truth and the nature of and justification for inferences.

Bateson (1980) suggests it is very difficult to distinguish between ontology and epistemology; however, the latter appears to be closely concerned with the establishment of truth and the justification of knowledge statements. He defines epistemology 'as the science that studies the process of knowing – the interaction of the capacity to respond to differences, on the one hand, with the material world in which those differences somehow originate, on the other' (Bateson, 1980).

It is a search for truth which drives activities to create knowledge. A dictionary definition of 'truth' includes 'conformity to fact or actuality', 'a statement proven to be or accepted as true' and 'that which is considered to be the supreme reality and to have the ultimate meaning and value of existence'. The *Internet Dictionary of Philosophy* (Fieser, 2004) identifies five theories of 'truth'. These include:

- *the coherence theory* which states that a coherent system of ideas is true;
- *the pragmatic theory* which suggests that the truth lies in a workable solution to a problem;

- *the semantic theory* which implies that truth, as a metaphysical concept, cannot be intelligently expressed in real language and requires a metalanguage;

- *the performative theory* which indicates that truth is whatever is agreed upon at a particular time and place;

- *the correspondence theory* which states that that which corresponds to reality is true (although reality can itself be a problematic concept).

There are several approaches to establishing the true nature of reality and of creating knowledge in this pursuit: these have been formalised over time into a range of academic disciplines which are typically categorised as the Humanities and Social Sciences (HSS) and the Natural Sciences (NS). C.P. Snow (1964) noted that these two cultures – of the humanities and the sciences and the accompanying division of research into qualitative and quantitative varieties – has created a cultural divide which entails serious consequences for creative, intellectual and everyday life.

These cultures have been classified in various ways. Biglan (1973) proposes three scales on which academic disciplines can differ: hard or soft, based on the extent of agreement on a paradigm within the discipline; pure or applied, based on emphasis on application; and life or non-life, based on concern with life systems. Becher (1989) subsequently identified four general disciplinary cultures (see Figure 3.1), ranging from the hard/pure culture of the sciences and the soft/pure culture of the humanities and the social sciences to the hard/applied culture of engineering and technology and the soft/applied cultures of the applied social sciences like education and social work.

This categorisation clearly indicates that NS and HSS are different: these differences can be articulated in various ways

	Hard (concrete)	Soft (abstract)
Pure (reflective)	Physics Chemistry Mathematics Geography	History Social sciences Psychology Political sciences
Applied (active)	Engineering Medicine	Law Library studies

Figure 3.1 A classification of scholarly disciplines (Becher, 1989)

(see Table 3.1). In general, humanistic qualitative research is thought to deal with the artistic expression of subjective emotions and opinions while scientific quantitative research deals with the precise description of objective facts and conditions.

These are well-accepted divisions and methods of examining reality and attempting to discover truth. Shepherd (1993) argues that major disciplines are characterised by different ontological cynosures that influence the interpretive frameworks of their practitioners: physicists see the world in terms of forces, chemists in terms of elements, biologists in terms of organisms, economists in terms of commodities and so forth. The effect is to make scientists from different disciplines see the world in fundamentally different ways (Shepherd, 1993). Do IPs see the world in terms of information or documents?

However, the use of the word 'cultures' by Snow deserves further attention. Culture is a word which cannot be explored at length here, but is understood to mean 'a set of important understandings that members of a community share in common – these include norms, values, attitudes, beliefs and paradigms'. A particular culture is normally associated with a particular community of people, who have

Table 3.1 Identification of differences between NS and HSS

Activity	NS	HSS
Knowledge creation	Observation and measurement	Assessment and evaluation
Work performed by	Teams	Individuals
Object of study	Objects, events and phenomena of all kinds in the natural world	Human beings, particularly their interactions and connections with others Products of imagination and ideas
Information flow	Invisible colleges	Loosely structured; individualistic
Information dissemination	Mostly journals	Mostly monographs
Nature of knowledge	Specific, objective, rationalist	Reiterative, holistic, qualities, interpretation
Boundaries between areas of study	Clearly marked	Often fuzzy
Methodology	Analysis/reductionist Opportunities for replication and generalisation Objectivity Hypothetico-deductive theory External law-like relations Exact	Synthesis/holistic Fewer opportunities for replication and generalisation Subjectivity Inductive Few laws

Table 3.1   (*continued*)

Language	Formal language and separation of facts from meaning (Lincoln and Guba, 1985) Definability and rigidity	Words themselves, and the meaning they convey, are contextualised, vague and varied Lack of rigid definability
Use of technology	Tools extensively used in NS	Tools seldom used in HSS
Gendered nature of knowledge	Masculinised	Feminised
Qualities	Abstract, theoretical, disembodied, emotionally detached, analytical, deductive, quantitative, atomistic and oriented toward values of control or domination	Concrete, practical, embodied, emotionally engaged, synthetic, intuitive, qualitative, relational and oriented toward values of social and individual care

common characteristics or interests, such as tribes, clubs, teams and so on.

Individuals belonging to such a community will create and construct knowledge through social interactions and subsequently share a similar understanding of reality, and often a similar language (although their membership of such a community might be temporary, and they might use a range of different languages in different situations, expressed by Bakhtin's notion of heteroglossia) (Voloshinov, 1994). Knowledge may only convey meaning and make sense against a particular cultural backdrop. For example, the notion of information (and its associated issues), as indicated previously by Agre (1995), can be socially constituted by TIPs as a cultural group. This suggests that the two areas of NS and HSS may have different ways of seeing or interpreting reality or truth if they constitute different cultures.

Kuhn indicated in *The Structure of Scientific Revolutions* (1970) that scientific knowledge is affected by the society (or culture) in which it is conducted. Kuhn concluded that scientific beliefs are influenced by social factors, as purely objective considerations seemed not to settle disputes between conflicting theories. This is supported by the Duhem-Quine thesis, which Putnam (1974) suggested proposes that an entire framework of beliefs is tested when a theory is tested: such testing does not occur in isolation. Multiple explanations of the same fact are ubiquitous in science – scientific theories are underdetermined by evidence because more than one theory fits any given set of evidence. There can even be multiple consistent logical systems. This thesis implies that factors other than evidence – presumably including social factors – determine the content of scientific theories, indicating accord with Kuhn.

Further, as Taylor notes, 'scientific facts are group constructs', suggesting that truth is performative and much of science comprises persuasion of others (noted by Rosenbaum, 1993). What passes as scientific knowledge varies and even changes radically as time passes. What is 'true' today may become mythology in the future.

Berger and Luckmann first explored the notion of the social construction of knowledge in 1966 in *The Social Construction of Reality*, positing that reality is sometimes viewed differently by different communities. Social constructionism is an interdisciplinary theoretical orientation which underpins a variety of approaches to the study of humans as social animals; these approaches include, but are not limited to, discourse analysis, deconstructionism and poststructuralism (Burr, 1995: 1). A social construct refers to a product created though human interaction. The social construction of reality means that all reality is produced through human interaction, through a particular relationship between the mind and the world. Characteristics of the social construction approach include:

- a critical stance towards taken-for-granted knowledge;
- a belief in historical and cultural specificity, whereby an understanding of the world is tied to culture and history;
- a belief that knowledge is sustained by social processes, that people construct knowledge between them in their daily social interactions;
- a belief that knowledge and social action go hand-in-hand;
- an understanding that there are numerous possible 'social constructions' of the world, and that each social construction brings with it a different human action (Burr, 1995: 3–5).

Two versions of social constructionism have been identified. In a 'weak' version of this theory, examples such as 'money' are given (e.g. Pinker, 2002: 202), as this concept is universally agreed on. 'Strong' social construction maintains that our understanding of reality is shaped by particular social circumstances customary at a particular time.

Reality is considered to exist only in our understanding of it. Strati observes that 'Information is notoriously influenced by the values and beliefs of the subjects that supply it and of those that gather it' (Strati, 1998). As Latour and Woolgar note, '... even though we construct society through and through, it lasts, it surpasses us, it dominates us, it has its own laws, it is as transcendent as Nature' (Latour and Woolgar, 1986: 27).

The social context in which knowledge creation is practised will affect what, and how, knowledge is created. If local culture influences what knowledges are developed, this could impede cross-community collaborative work and knowledge sharing because of loss of meaning between individual frames of reference. The idea that social phenomena do not exist as natural events or objects in the world, but are brought into existence by human social activity, has important implications for how they should be studied. Frohmann (1994) remarks that this theoretical approach is underutilised in LIS.

Foucault and discourse

Foucault introduced the concept of 'discourses' to explain the systems of knowledge, meaning and truth that define and organise the world according to specific points of view, and how the structure of contemporary thought is shaped by social institutions and practices. While Kuhn's view suggests a form of social construction of knowledge, Foucault maintains that there is no fixed or definitive structure of identity or practice, as these are the result of historically specific discourses.

Discourses are ways of viewing or understanding reality at particular times. Burr defines discourse as 'a set of meanings, metaphors, representations, images, stories, statements and so on that in some way together produce a particular version of events. It refers to a particular picture that is painted of an event (or person or class of persons), a particular way of representing it or them in a particular light' (Burr, 1995: 48).

> Discourses, in Foucault's work, are ways of constituting knowledge, together with the social practices, forms of subjectivity and power relations which inhere in such knowledges and the relations between them. Discourses are more than ways of thinking and producing meaning. They constitute the 'nature' of the body, unconscious and conscious mind and the emotional life of the subjects they seek to govern. (Jordan and Weedon, 1987: 108)

Foucault explores the ways in which particular discourses create their own definitions of knowledge and truth, and defines an episteme as a system of discourses which comes to dominate a particular historical era. Such an episteme will inform the way in which thinking is done and knowledge produced during a particular time, which subsequently can change; an episteme is discontinuous. In so doing, he reveals the 'other side' of history, by describing how certain assumptions effectively suppress variations (or deviations) from the prevailing episteme.

In Foucault's view, knowledge is inextricably connected to power, such that the words are often combined as power/ knowledge. Knowledge is inherent in systems of thought (epistemes) which become dominant through being socially legitimated and institutionalised, and serve the aims of power and social domination.

> The working hypothesis will be this: power relations ... do not only play with respect to knowledge a facilitating or obstructive role; ... power and knowledge are not linked together solely by the play of interests or ideologies ... No body of knowledge can be formed without a system of communications, records, accumulation and displacement which is in itself a form of power and which is linked, in its existence

> and functioning, to the other forms of power. Conversely, no power can be exercised without the extraction, appropriation, distribution or retention of knowledge. On this level, there is not knowledge on the one side and society on the other ... but only the fundamental forms of knowledge/power. (Foucault, 1972: 131)

He first described this as 'archaeology' (in *Archaeology of Knowledge*, 1972), a term which indicates 'practices that systematically form the objects of which they speak' (Foucault, 1972: 49): they are a particular set of beliefs, philosophical assumptions and opinions that are found in a certain group of people, different from the formal knowledge of the group or profession. He holds that power/ knowledge moulds not only those in power, but particularly the discursively disempowered. Feenberg (1991) argues that Foucault's view of oppression is more closely linked to effective techniques of hegemony[4] than false ideologies.

Truth, in Foucault's view, cannot be separated from the discursive formation of a discipline. Davies and Harre claim that: 'To know anything is to know in terms of one or more discourses' (Davies and Harre, 1990: 45). Foucault argues that objectivity is suspect, and in his many works he identifies three ways in which subjects can be objectified: 'dividing practices', where marginalised groups are dominated through the mediation of science and the practice of social exclusion; 'scientific classification', where various modes of enquiry try to give themselves the status of the sciences; and 'subjectification', or the process of self-formation in which a person plays an active part in transformation into a social subject. Derrida took this work further and, through deconstruction, attempted to identify the definitions of truth that have structured such discourses.

Others agree with the relationship between power and knowledge. Mannheim (1936) first indicated that granting the truth of any knowledge claim benefits some people at the expense of others, and thus the process of epistemic justification is a way of distributing or enforcing power. Pahre further suggests that the creation of disciplines has served particular power interests at various times, and disciplinary boundaries would almost certainly be different were they to be re-established today (Pahre, 1996).

What makes this a particularly complicated matter is that while philosophical, sociological, economic, techno-logical, organisational and psychological theories can be explored in order to articulate differences, at the same time it is argued that the ways in which such knowledge and theories are developed is core to a metatheory for the IPs. The IPs might well be influenced by changing paradigms, discourses, norms and values and their interactions: simultaneously, it is precisely how knowledge is created and produced, how information is represented and makes meaning, and how information is used in cultures, soci-eties and organisations, that should constitute information metatheory.

Dominant epistemes

While the differences between NS and HSS disciplines were discussed above based on how research is done in these categories, we can now, using a discursive approach, identify two epistemes, or systems of discourses – the modernist and the postmodernist.

Enlightenment or modernist epistemology

Since the Age of Enlightenment in the seventeenth century, the modernist episteme has dominated knowledge creation. Until recently, the fact that science was solely responsible for the production, evaluation, canonisation and revision of the knowledge it generated was virtually a characteristic of modernity (for example, Luhmann, 1990). Science is seen as constituting an authoritative body of knowledge which combats superstitions and mythologies and is able to discover the truth.

There are distinctive characteristics of the modernist epistemology, of which science is taken as an example. The first characteristic is that of exteriorisation. Only those things which can be experienced through the five senses are understood to have importance. There is traditionally little concern with the unseen or the undetected, although this has changed as research tools have become more specialised and accurate, extending the range of human senses.

Phenomena are observed in a purportedly objective, detached and rationalist way; knowledge is acquired through a subject, who is the knower, and the object, which becomes known. Hekman notes that: 'Feminists reject the opposition of the subject and object because inherent in this opposition is the assumption that only men can be subjects, and, hence, knowers' (Hekman, 1990).

Secondly, these 'things' exist only if they are measurable, even though the measuring implements may be inadequate or faulty. Measurements are typically expressed in numbers. The importance of measurement is emphasised by the apocryphal comment by Lord Kelvin: 'When you can measure what you are speaking about and express it in numbers, you know something about it, but when you cannot measure it, when you cannot express it in numbers, your knowledge is of a meagre and unsatisfactory kind' (Cleverdon and Keen, 1966: 31). The sciences depend on quantification in establishing 'truth' as that which cannot be measured is understood to lack veracity.

Thirdly, the phenomena are categorised and named. A substantial part of scientific research sets out to establish what relationships exist between phenomena. Phenomena are incorporated into an order, commonly hierarchical, which demonstrates these relationships, so phenomena are represented as being superior or subordinate to one another (even though this may be based on spurious principles of division). Melville Dewey's classification scheme is a well-known example. He divided the world of knowledge arbitrarily into ten sections, and each of these categories is further divided into ten subcategories, and so on. Every 'thing' must fit into one of these categories. By definition, they cannot fit into more than one category, as a phenomenon is 'either/or', and cannot have more than one simultaneous feature upon which to base categorisation.

Accepting such a structure means tolerating inconsistencies, and it also carries the implication of seeing phenomena in terms of dualisms or as dichotomies, as 'things' are either one thing or another. What is interesting about dualisms is that generally one of the pair is perceived as privileged – and this is generally associated with masculine attributes, goodness, strength and so forth.

Such categorisation of phenomena or objects implies importance or lack of it, and in so doing, embodies a particular world-view and can be hegemonic, implying that all there is to know is known. In the Dewey Decimal Classification (DDC) system, 'Australia' shares about as much conceptual space as all extra-terrestrial life forms (obviously anticipating there are not too many of these). However, things North

American, and seen from a male, Anglo-Saxon, Judeo-Christian, English-speaking perspective, occupy the vast majority of the conceptual space in this knowledge format.

The Enlightenment or modernist episteme, through its emphasis on objectivity and its alleged neutrality of values, has led many to suppose that its processes can establish the truth about reality. 'Positivism' refers to a positive evaluation of science and scientific method. Five central aspects are applauded – objectivity, hypothetico-deductive theory, external law-like relations, exact and formal language, and separation of facts from meaning (Lincoln and Guba, 1985). The great success of the natural sciences has been based not on scrupulous utilisation of all available relevant information about natural phenomena but on systematic simplification, idealisation, abstraction, approximation and the concomitant ignoring of very large quantities of admittedly relevant information (Wilson, 1995).

Problems with the modernist episteme range from the selection of what to look for (and what is seen) to the use of unreliable or inadequate measuring tools, and include Heisenberg's 'uncertainty principle', which suggests that not even physical objects are inert in and untouched by observational processes. It is by no means certain that an autonomous, objective world exists independently, and can be interpreted independently, by humans who are value-free, and that this same objective world will in turn determine how we think about things.

From Mannheim and Kuhn onwards, the influence of culture has been observed in scientific practice. Critiques from several disciplines have attacked science for its notion of truth and rationality as well as the alleged objectivity of scientific method. All this criticism has established that science is a social process, that scientific method is little short of a myth, and that scientific knowledge is in fact manufactured according to prevailing power structures. The representation of science as a modernist enterprise carries with it the ideas of progress, capitalism, technological superiority and other ideologies. Vogel has suggested that the

> ... 'nature' investigated by natural science is a constituted nature, constituted not by some abstract species-interest in prediction and control, but by a complex set of scientific practices that instantiate what Kuhn called a 'paradigm'. The 'nature' of natural science in this sense is a social construct, constituted in and through the interaction not only among those who investigate it but also within the wider community as well. (Vogel, 1995: 30)

The biggest dilemma of the modernist episteme, which privileges the rationalist, scientific method, is that it does not seem able to explain contemporary phenomena. New developments in mathematics suggest that there are serious limits to our scientific knowledge. The merging theories of chaos and complexity demolish the notion of control and certainty in science. Both theories promise a revolution in science based on notions of holism, interconnection and order out of chaos. As Barnes and Bloor put it, 'there are no context-free or super-cultural norms of rationality' (Barnes and Bloor, 1982: 27).

Postmodernist epistemology

Postmodernism has become, over the past two decades, a prevalent theory used to help understand contemporary society. Defining postmodernism is repeatedly shown to be a difficult task, which may originate in the diversity of post-modern approaches to the study of culture and the human condition. Despite many elements of postmodern theory which are discipline-specific, there are a number of general precepts of postmodernism which define the boundaries of this epistemology. Hekman (1990: 3–12) succinctly notes these:

- Postmodernism challenges modernist assumptions of culture and human behaviour. This includes questioning the belief that the scientific method of the natural sciences is the only paradigm of knowledge.

- A rejection of absolutism in favour of relativism. There is no single, absolute, objective truth, but multiple, subjective truths relative to one's social context.

- The belief that knowledge is interpretive and not founded in the 'truth' of grand metanarratives; this includes an examination of the production of meaning in shaping human existence.

- A rejection of modernism's privileging of rational discourse (and universal reason) as the sole avenue to 'truth', in favour of alternative forms of knowing that are partial, historical and social.

- A rejection of dominant cultural understandings (especially euro- and andro-centric notions of knowledge) in favour of multiple cultural perspectives – this includes the belief that no single tradition or story can speak for the entirety of human experience.

Postmodernism allows for the disappearance of self (as opposed to the power of the knower) and indicates an end to universal and hegemonic definitions, discourses and world views. Lemert (1990: 52–3) has made a useful distinction between two strands of postmodernism:

- *Radical postmodernism* constitutes a nihilistic approach to the world which believes that modernity has been overthrown by a new social arrangement in which reality is a virtual reality, mediated through popular culture. Here, there is little basis for defining any idea as any more real than another.

■ *Strategic postmodernism* believes that modernism still holds a degree of social power, and that its own precepts must be used against it to effect social change. Here, the goal is to subvert modern culture and overcome its denial of difference.

The first of these approaches is evident in the work of such postmodern thinkers such as Baudrillard (1994), for whom the modern world has given way to the postmodern, resulting in a simulated reality that is mediated through cultural artefacts; an individual's sense of the world (of his or her 'reality') is constructed through the images one sees on television, in films, in newspapers (which he calls hyper-reality and simulacra).

Strategic postmodernism is evidenced in the work of such writers as Foucault (1970) and Jacques Derrida (1982), who focus on rewriting, reworking and subverting elements of modernity. Subversion of the dominant culture occurs in order to privilege previously marginalised perspectives.

The postmodernist view defines all knowledge as interpretative, as situated within a particular reality. For Gibbons et al. (1994), postmodernism indicates a new mode of knowledge production, Mode 2. Mode 1, the traditional form of knowledge production, is the modernist, scientific approach.

Postmodernity has led to a growing indeterminacy of disciplinary boundaries, and an emphasis on contextualisation, interdisciplinary work, and heterogeneity of forms and sites of knowledge production. There are no universal absolutes, but there is a focus on process rather than product, on becoming rather than being, and the dynamic rather than the static. Nothing is neutral, impartial or objective – everything is created for a set purpose, and there is no ultimate truth (Cook, 2000a).

An important tool of analysis in postmodernism is Lyotard's concept of the 'metanarrative' – a theory claiming to provide universal explanations and to be universally valid. This explains the dominance of the Enlightenment epistemology across many fields. Postmodernism, however, allows a simultaneity of existence. It permits polyvocality, and delights in deconstructing the 'grand narrative' of Enlightenment thought. Another postmodernist process is that of 'decentring', which undermines centres of authority and meaning privileged by the Enlightenment metanarrative.

What is particularly interesting about the postmodernist episteme is its ubiquity in a number of fields of knowledge. As Appignanesi and Garratt observe, 'What we have is one of those rare occasions in history when science and art arrive independently at complementary attitudes' (Appignanesi and Garratt, 1995: 16).

Memetics (Dawkins, 1990) explains the similarity between models of understanding being constructed more or less simultaneously in a diverse range of disciplines, such as feminism and information retrieval. A meme is a self-spreading thought or idea, but does not, according to Lynch, 'create some kind of grand unification of the social sciences ...' (Lynch, 1996). It describes the event of an idea acting like a virus, infecting a number of hosts.

Heisenberg introduced the Uncertainty Principle in 1927: the impossibility of predicting both the mass and velocity of a particle at any given moment, so that there is always uncertainty in the simultaneous measurements of the position of a particle. He stated this as: 'The more precisely the position is determined, the less precisely the momentum is known in this instant, and vice versa' (Cassidy, 1992). Uncertainty introduced the notion of relativism, more fully developed by Einstein, which supplanted Newtonian physics. Einstein embarked on a quest to demonstrate Unified Field Theory – the Theory of Everything.

Capra wrote of the necessity to cross disciplinary boundaries in *The Tao of Physics*, in which he compares research into subatomic physics with eastern mysticism.[5] It is hard to imagine a connection between two more disparate thought trails. Physicists found that it was difficult, if not impossible, to understand the relationship between time and space using traditional empiricist and rationalist methods.

An element of repetition can be discovered in many bodies of literature, with parallel shifts in their discourses from modernist to postmodernist positions. These simultaneous paradigm shifts result in apparently diverse disciplines converging. The first striking example is art, where realism ended with Cezanne, Picasso, Leger and Braque and their development of Cubism. Cubism recognises that each object has multiple simultaneous viewpoints, and that each viewer has an individual picture of the object, or understanding of reality. Other examples are found in cosmology, organisational sciences, music (John Cage), architecture (in particular the work of Charles Jencks), literary theory, feminism (Hekman's work is interesting here) and philosophy (Foucault, Derrida, Bourdieu, Barthes et al.).

> Those working in computing will know well the ideas of Nelson and van Dam; those working in literary and cultural theory will know equally well the ideas of Derrida and Barthes. All four, like many others who write on hypertext or literary theory, argue that we must abandon conceptual systems founded upon ideas of center, margin, hierarchy and linearity and replace

them with ones of multilinearity, nodes, links and networks. (Landow, 1992)

Dreher has created an interesting model (see Table 3.2) which distinguishes between a rational, empiricist or scientific approach to knowledge creation, and compares this with a postmodernist, social constructivist stance, which compares interestingly with the divisions between NS and HSS.

LIS – an art or a science?

Not only are divisions between disciplines within the field of human knowledge artificial and inaccurate in the light of our continuing exploration and experience, but such divisions embody cultural and societal views which seek to maintain the status quo. The NS, because of their association with the modernist episteme, are both privileged and masculinised areas of knowledge, and enjoy an exalted social status. The HSS are acknowledged as 'different', and traditionally have been constituted as a disprivileged, marginalised 'other'. As the IPs, particularly in their embodiment as places of enculturation and education, have long been identified as a social science (and located in HSS in universities), they have suffered a more lowly status.

In an effort to overcome this, the HSS, and the IPs, have attempted to follow the NS model in order to gain both credibility and funding. The first movement in this direction was the work done at the Graduate Library School at the University of Chicago, established in 1926, which drew on the philosophy of John Dewey whose work on the science of education was influential. Both Butler and Waples were academics at this school and Shera was a graduate. As Ellis

Table 3.2 Dreher's model (Dreher, 1997: 68)

Level	Positivism	Constructivism
Ontology (being)	Realist – reality exists and is driven by immutable natural laws and mechanisms. Knowledge of these entities is conventionally summarised in the form of time- and context-free generalisations.	Relativist – realities exist in the form of multiple mental constructions, socially and experientially based, local and specific, depending for their form and content on the person who holds them.
Epistemology (knowing)	Dualist/objectivist – it is both possible and essential for the enquirer to adopt a distant, non-interactive posture.	Subjectivist – enquire and enquired into are fused into a single (monistic) entity. Findings are literally the creation of the process of interaction between the two.
Methodology (doing)	Experimental/ manipulative – questions and/or hypotheses are stated in advance in propositional form and subjected to experimental tests under carefully controlled conditions.	Hermeneutic, dialectic – individual constructions are elicited and refined hermeneutically, and compared and contrasted dialectically, with the aim of generating one or a few constructions on which there is substantial consensus.

(1996) notes, the primary objective of the early research-ers in LIS, such as Cranfield tests (known as Cranfield I and II), conducted by Cyril Cleverdon and associates in the mid-1950s, was to establish information retrieval as a modern scientific discipline.

> The principal methodological assumption, and the key to the enterprise, was that the study of the interaction of the entities was to be based on the application of the scientific method, and that the interaction between the devices was to be understood entirely in quantitative terms in relation to the newly conceived measures of recall, precision and fallout. These measures were themselves derived from the basic quantity, or criterion of measurement, of relevance. (Ellis, 1996: 24)

These preliminary empirical experiments were highly controlled and artificial, based largely on a prescribed and finite body of documents containing information described by indexing languages (a form of metadata). Effectiveness was measured in two dimensions: the extent to which known 'relevant' documents were retrieved, and how well retrieval of 'non-relevant' documents was suppressed. The former measure (recall) assesses the comprehensiveness of a search and the latter (precision) assesses accuracy.

Characteristics of the Cranfield tests, which became archetypal, are: (a) a set of test document collections; (b) laboratory testing; (c) measurements of recall versus precision (Harter, 1996: 157). It was assumed epistemologically that information retrieval (IR) devices could be studied in isolation from their operational environment. Such a mechanistic model describes an ideal information-seeking situation and suggests that information retrieval systems operate like physical systems. This endeavour received approval from the traditional IPs as it was believed that this might improve the stature and image of the profession and is evidenced by the emergence of the phrase 'information science' which developed at this time, more or less simultaneously with computer science.

However, these tests were inherently flawed due to confusion about what was actually being tested and measured. Even though 'recall', 'precision' and 'fallout' continue to be used today, these are predicated upon the assumption of an agreed concept of relevance. The Cranfield tests assumed relevance comprised matching the terms entered at searching with the terms used by the creator of the document or document surrogate.

The focus of measuring relevance has now shifted toward 'user-based' or 'user-centred' relevance, acknowledging the concept that users' determination of 'relevance' is a more accurate tool for measuring IR systems, as it is based on 'real' information needs. Schamber, Eisenberg and Nilan reviewed the literature on relevance and concluded that relevance is a 'topical, user-oriented, multi-dimensional, cognitive and dynamic' concept (Schamber, Eisenberg and Nilan, 1990: 755), with the result that relevance judgements are probably dependent on a vast array of situational dimensions which would be difficult to take into account in system design (Hert, 1997: 9). Being subjective, it cannot be measured absolutely but only relatively, and thus it is difficult to force the IPs into a scientific tradition. Mizzaro (1997) has provided a most useful literature review of relevance.

Neill regards information management as an art. He points out the importance of expression, language and communication, particularly as there is no scientific construction of knowledge (Neill, 1992: xiii). Using language involves the human attributes of interpretation, understanding, intuition, imagination, intelligence, personality and character which define information management as an art rather than a science (Neill, 1991: 148).

As the study of information has thus far not provided a cohesive or core theory, as noted, there is no identifiable paradigm or episteme within which disciplinary knowledge is created. In addition, the information professions must, of necessity, be associated with knowledge and information in all disciplines, and not just those in either HSS or NS. With the present mythology, however, a large number of practising IPs are drawn from HSS, rather than NS, creating an interesting paradox.

This puts the IPs at a great disadvantage, as defining and explaining their role is, at the best of times, problematic. Modes of knowledge production are changing, which has relevance not only for the construction of disciplinary knowledge, but is also necessary for the understanding of information work itself. In addition, the IPs are located in a changing context, which needs to be responded to in an appropriate fashion, which is difficult without a theoretical base. The context itself is creating changes within the IPs.

Notes

1. Brittain (1995) indicated that only 20 per cent of LIS graduates end up in the profession, and that 75 per cent of the potential employment market required skills, knowledge and experience that were not provided in LIS schools.
2. ALARM has published an interesting cross-disciplinary competence profile.
3. For example, Jarvelin and Vakkari reported theory use in only 10 per cent of empirical studies published in 1985. Julien, focusing on the information needs and uses literature published from 1990 to 1994, reported an increase in theory use in that 28 per cent of the 165 articles sampled were theoretically grounded, meaning that they were 'based on a coherent and explicit framework of assumptions, definitions and propositions that, taken together, have some explanatory power' (Julien, 1996:

56). In a more recent related study, Julien and Duggan (2000) found that only 18.3 per cent of the 300 research studies sampled from 1984 to 1989 and 1995 to 1998 were theoretically based (McKechnie, Pettigrew and Joyce, 2001: 48).

4. Antonio Gramsci's Theory of Hegemony states that: 'the group in power in society always insists that intellectual discussion shall take place in the kind of language which it uses, which it understands, and which represents its way of seeing, interpreting and dominating the world'.

5. Capra's argument is best explained in *The Tao of Physics* (1975), in which he explores the connections between Eastern mysticism and modern physics. Here, the unity of all things is expressed, and also the relative relationship between things.

4

Changing context

The more it changes ...

Changing contexts or environments demand responses from individuals and organisations, and professions are not immune. Ostler and Dahlin note that if

> ... the social and economic conditions remained the same [as in Dewey's time], the profession would enjoy some degree of success and acceptance; but if conditions were to change, there was no unified body of theory to provide 'conceptual lenses' to look at a completely new set of problems and suggest ways to deal with them. (Ostler and Dahlin, 1995: 683)

Changes require new ways of doing things, new approaches to problem-solving and even new ways of thinking.

An historical account documenting the changes in libraries, technology and information is beyond the scope of this work, although some aspects are commented on. There are, however, at least three other ways of examining the context of the TIPs.

The first approach is systems theory, which indicates that the nature of the environment demands a response from an open system to ensure its survival and success. Open systems theory was first developed by Emery and Trist in 1965, who recognised organisations as open systems. A system is a group of items or activities which interact and are interdependent, but which are motivated by a common set of goals, thus forming a functional whole. Outside the boundaries of the system, there is a sudden change in purpose. Systems are embedded within environments, with which they constantly engage. Open systems theory recognises the active role of the environment in relation to a system's survival and success; a system likewise can have an interactive relationship with an environment and cause changes within it. Emery and Trist noted that an environment can change over time, and such changes affect systems within it (Emery and Trist, 1965).

Environments can be described using a number of criteria. These include the amount of change, how rapidly it occurs, how many elements of change are involved, the strength of their effect upon a system, and so on. Emery and Trist thus characterised four different types of environment: the *placid random* environment, the *placid clustered* environment, the *disturbed reactive* environment and the *turbulent* environment (Emery and Trist, 1972). Malhotra identified a fifth: the *wicked* environment, characterised by discontinuous change and imposing 'the need for variety and complexity of the interpretations that are necessary for deciphering the multiple world views of the uncertain and unpredictable future' (Malhotra, 1997).

Using systems theory in this context is particularly apposite as it supports cybernetics, a branch of information theory, which assists the analysis of complex problems, identifying the sources and effects of change within the environment and relationships between system and environment.

The second approach is contextualism, which locates an object, event or individual within a context in order to better understand it. Contextualism is used to understand linguistics, music, architecture, organisational change, philosophy and the social sciences, and can be used for analysis as well as understanding the relationship between objects and their environment, each other and among the various components of the object.

The third approach is habitus, which describes the culture and nature of the profession, and how it perceives its environment as a result. The habitus of the TIPs, as noted, has been largely concerned with the management of tangible documents, and the techniques and procedures which are associated with this, with the aim of social upliftment. Social needs vary greatly, subject to spatio-temporal constraints among others; added to this, social need and upliftment is extremely difficult to determine, particularly using quantitative methodologies.

The IPs are located within multiple, intersecting, nested layers of context, which include cultural (philosophical, epistemological, paradigmatic), social (norms and values), professional, technological, organisational (information ecology), situational (immediate information use environment) and individual (cognitive and affective abilities) layers which act simultaneously. There are relationships of various kinds between such layers of context; boundaries are not always clear as there are associations and influences between them, and each of these will have different effects upon the professions. All of these, as well as the interactions between them, cause change. The layers of context and the elements within them are, as Nelson has noted, 'intertwingled'.[1]

Technology as a force for change

Technology is often picked out as the single driving force for change in the TIPs. The word 'technology', from the Greek 'tekhne' meaning an art or craft, first meant 'the systematic treatment of an art'. During the mid-nineteenth century, technology came to mean specifically practical arts or manufacture. The word is now used to describe a diverse collection of phenomena, including tools, instruments, machines, organisations, methods and techniques – and sometimes all of these.

There are a number of different ways of examining the relationship between technology and society. Most traditional theories on the nature of and relationship between technology and society are divided into two classic approaches, namely technological determinism and social constructionism. However, in both cases there have been significant advances over the years in the direction of integrating relevant factors from both social and materials realms. As a result, at least three major approaches can now be identified.

Firstly, there is the determinist approach, which sees technology as changing and shaping society. Secondly, there are those theories which see technology as passive tools, which might be used, or not used, in particular ways by humans. Lastly, there are those theories which see technology and its use as being shaped by a particular society or culture, and thus being an extension or reinforcement of an existing status quo.

Technological determinism

It is interesting to note a comment made by Leslie White in 1949:

> We may view a cultural system as a series of three horizontal strata: the technological layer on the bottom, the philosophical on the top, the sociological stratum in between ... The technological system is

basic and primary. Social systems are functions of technologies; and philosophers express technological forces and reflect social systems. The technological factor is therefore the determinant of a cultural system as a whole. It determines the form of social systems, and technology and society together determine the content and orientation of philosophy. (White, 1949)

Technological determinism (TD) describes an assumption that ICTs are the primary cause of major social changes, and have the power to transform the whole of society at every level. A wide range of social and cultural phenomena are seen as shaped by technology, and human factors and social arrangements are seen as secondary in influence.

It posits that technology exerts a unidirectional influence over humans and organisations similar to the laws of physical sciences, notably in a cause and effect relationship that is associated with scientific research. TD illustrates a form of reductionism, where a complex whole is reduced to one feature – change agent. This is then reified, and in this manner an otherwise abstract concept assumes tangible properties, which are usually uniform and homogenous, and becomes autonomous.

Rather than being a product or part of society, technology is considered independent, controlling, determining, generating and perpetuating itself in a relentless fashion. The use of deterministic language is revealing, as Chandler indicates.

The assumption of technological determinism can usually be easily spotted in frequent references to the 'impact' of technological 'revolutions' which 'led to' or 'brought about', 'inevitable', 'far-reaching', 'effects' or 'consequences'. This sort of language gives such writing an animated, visionary, prophetic tone which many people find inspiring and convincing. (Chandler, 1995)

Technological determinists maintain that single technologies have the power to, and indeed do, change society. Marshall McLuhan (an archetypal technological determinist) described *inter alia* the connection between feudalism and the stirrup, and suggested that this modification to riding horses led to a change in the nature of warfare, which resulted in the reorganisation of society.

The deterministic view assumes that technology possesses its own logic, and develops along certain paths that represent natural technological choices. It also implies a suspension of ethical judgement or social control. Individuals and society are seen as serving the requirements of a technological system which shapes their activities, and we become 'innocent victims' (Chandler, 1995).

Feenberg, in *Critical Theory of Technology* (1991), claims that theories of the relationship between society and technology fall into one of two major categories: the instrumental theory and the substantive theory. The substantive theories argue 'that technology constitutes a new type of cultural system that restructures the entire social world as an object of control' (Pacey, 1997: 7), and its best known authors are Ellul and Heidegger.

Ellul (1954) identified three milieux, of which the technological is the most recent, being preceded by the natural and social milieux. A milieu is a context which both makes demands on us and provides us with a means of survival, and shapes society by influencing social groups and interactions. Technology is not simply a means to an end but an environment and a way of life: this is its substantive impact. The dominant milieu causes previous problems to become obsolete. Whether one believes technology to be good or bad is immaterial, as the nature of technology is so encompassing that it defies judgement, and will continue 'subjugating our humanity'. Ellul sees humans as virtually helpless in the technological milieu and the 'value' of efficiency drives everything.

Like Ellul, Heidegger views technology as all-embracing, and uses the term 'Gestell' (framing) to express this concept – technology is not neutral but frames the world. Heidegger's concept of technology is not defined by things or processes: '. . . technology's essence is nothing technological' (Heidegger, 1977: 4) – it is a mode of human existence which is affected by technology. The 'essence of technology' is dangerous as it can transform and even distort human actions, including how we know and think (Heidegger, in Heim, 1993: 61).

A facile connection is often made between social progress and technological progress, as implied by Bell's work (Bell, 1974), although he is not alone. Tools are seen to mark the transition from a traditional society to a modern society. Slack and Fejes (1987) note Ravault's comment that modern societies are seen as 'better': they are based on scientific, objective and technological knowledge, and rational decision-making. On the other hand, (inferior) traditional societies are seen to be based on intuition, value judgements, religious beliefs, prejudice and ideology (Ravault, in Slack and Fejes, 1987: 9). Modernism is associated with progress.

Pacey believes it is simplistic to consider that technology can only lead to greater progress and efficiency. According to Pacey, 'a technocratic value system . . . gives rise to what is often called a "technocratic" outlook that is single-mindedly insistent on an unambiguous view of progress, of problem-solving, and of values' (Pacey, 1997: 127). However, society is so complex that technological development cannot be linear and continuous. He notes, firstly, that progress is typically measured quantitatively, and qualitative issues and developments are ignored as these are not associated with 'progress'. Secondly, while the objective of the Industrial Revolution was to speed up manual work, there were many other results of mechanisation, including fragmentation of labour and deskilling; technologies almost always have unforeseen uses and consequences. Lastly, progress is neither linear nor continuous, but complex and diverse.

Humans are active participants in social change, and hegemony can be avoided by interactivity with technological processes. Technological development is not separate from society, and technological artefacts cannot predict their social consequences. 'Technologies have limited agency', notes Balsamo (1996: 123), while Castells maintains that 'The "technology push" approach, which associates the development of the information society with a technical revolution of production, can only insufficiently comprehend the fundamental economic and social changes caused by this transformation process' (Castells, 1997: 30).

The prevailing stance in the TIP literature is that of TD: technology is seen as creating change in the profession as it exists 'out there' and must be accommodated within the practice of the profession, regardless. A critical approach which examines what technologies are useful, why and how they can be used, and what the outcomes might be in relation to the aims of the profession and the information needs of the society or organisation they serve appears to be lacking.

Neutral view

Other approaches to the relationship between technology and society and the work of the TIPs are seldom considered. One of these is a neutral view, which sees technologies as tools to work with. In *Communication as Culture*, Carey wrote: 'Electronics is neither the arrival of apocalypse nor the dispensation of grace. Technology is technology; it is a means for communication and transportation over space, and nothing more' (Carey, 1992: 139).

From this perspective, technology is a visible machine or apparatus. The neutral approach falls into the category which Feenberg identified as the 'instrumental theory', based on the idea that technologies are 'tools' or instruments which serve the purposes of their users. 'Technology is deemed "neutral", without valuative content of its own' (Feenberg, 1991: 5); as an instrument, technology is neither good nor bad, and can be used for both purposes, noting that the 'price for the achievement of environmental, ethical or religious goals ... is reduced efficiency' (Feenberg, 1991: 6). The issue here is, how can technologies best support the work of the TIPs beyond mere efficiency? Can ICTs expand the role of the TIPs to cope with the IS?

Technology shaped by society

The view least explored by the TIPs is that there exists the possibility to make choices regarding the use of technology, and even the opportunity to participate in designing it or modifying it for particular applications.

There are at least five bodies of theory related to the mutual interaction of influence between technology and society, although there are overlaps between them. These are the socio-technical perspective (STP), the actor-network theory (ANT), the social shaping of technology (SST), the social construction of technology (SCOT) and social constructivism. Of these, SCOT assumes arguably the most political view, while the other four are more neutral.

The socio-technical perspective (STP) is situated between TD, which sees technology as driving changes in society, and SCOT, which sees all technology as a product of social activity, usually playing a role in the preservation of or increase in the power of particular groups or ideologies. This outlook suggests that it is possible for people to gain control over, and even influence, technological development through their interactions with the technology: the technology is constructed thorough the choices and decisions made by people.

The main proponents of the actor-network theory (ANT) are Latour, Law and Callon. Frohmann has defined an actor network as 'simultaneously an actor whose activity is networking heterogeneous elements and a network that is able to redefine and transform what it is made of' (Frohmann, 1997). The network elements are seen as 'hybrids' or 'quasi-objects' which involve science, technology and social relations, and ANT does not reduce the explanations of technological use to particular social, natural or discursive areas as these are already present in the network. Frohmann explains that ANT focuses on the ability of the actors to manipulate the network and technological practice rather than on the creation of technologies (Frohmann, 1997).

The social shaping of technology (SST) approach is influenced by ANT, and examines two aspects of TD. Technology is not seen as neutral, but it also does not determine social outcomes because of the possibility of human intervention. Technological development takes place within society, and is seen to be shaped by its context, comprising a variety of ideological and cultural practices. There is no reification of technology, which develops according to its own logic and agenda; instead, humans, who are themselves responsive to and products of particular environments, can play a role in determining technological development and outcomes.

Users shape technology to their own ends, and this accounts for different technological styles in different organisational or national settings, as technology is used differently. Kling and McKim noted that:

> The configuration of socio-technological ensembles is driven by a series of operational choices (conscious and unconscious) made both during the creation and during the implementation of the technology. The configurable nature of many technologies – particularly ICT – enables this shaping to continue during their use. (Kling and McKim, 1999)

Sawyer and Rosenbaum (2000) describe how ICTs do not exist in social or technological isolation, but are located within social and organisational contexts:

> ... ICTs can most usefully be conceptualised as 'socio-technical systems' composed of an interrelated and interdependent mix of people, their social and work practices, the norms of use, hardware and software, the support systems that aid users, the maintenance systems that keep the ICTs operating: this is what Kling and Scacchi (1982) have called the 'web of computing'. (Sawyer and Rosenbaum, 2000)

TIPs have largely exhibited a reluctance to become involved with the design and interpretation of the technologies that they use, and their interest usually extends only to how they are able to incorporate them into practice. The possibilities provided by the incorporation of technologies into information management places and practices have typically not been explored. For example, being released from many manual tasks such as circulation of materials and cataloguing might have led to the development of more customised services, but instead the result has been fewer information professionals being employed.

The social construction of technology (SCOT) conceptual framework was developed largely by Bijker (Bijker, Hughes and Pinch, 1989; Bijker and Law, 1992; Bijker, 1995), and it explains how the cultural, social and historical forces influence the design, development and transformation of technology. It appears to be in direct opposition to the TD view, as it explicitly rejects the notion of technology as an exogenous variable to which society and individuals must adapt.

Technologies are seen as social constructions, the outcome of negotiations between relevant social groups within a 'technological frame' (that is, a socially constructed reality or intellectual system within which a device or project is set) (Bijker, 1993). Technology is seen as a product of the society which created it, constructed by society in order to replicate certain aspects of the society and to further society's aims.

An associated theory is that of social constructivism (SC). Here, the focus is specifically on traditional scientific practice based on rationality. It assumes that all knowledge is constructed, including notions of race, criminality, gender, truth, reality and fact (*Wordiq.com*, 2004). SC identities technology as neutral, but its effects are not direct as there is opportunity for human choice and intervention. Simultaneously, the theory argues that technology itself is not neutral, but is itself determined by social, ecological and political factors which are constructed by humans. Frohmann regards social constructivism as an approach in which

> ... scientific and technological outcomes are not solutions to uniquely scientific and technical problems existing apart from social processes, but are instead negotiated social processes as thoroughly social as the outcomes of political campaigns located firmly in their cultural, political and economic contexts. (Frohmann, 1994)

He considers that the useful ideas which SC provides are:

(1) science and technology do not inhabit realms distinct from the social;
(2) technological systems are networks of heterogeneous elements, maintained in an uneasy equilibrium; and
(3) the success of technological systems depends upon adjustments of supporting social macro-structures. (Frohmann, 1994)

Social constructivism emphasises that: 'Members of a society together invent the properties of the world' and reality 'does not exist prior to its social invention' (Kim, 2001). Knowledge is therefore a human product, a result of humans' attempt to make sense of reality.

Once again, there are 'weak' and 'strong' versions. The 'weak' version of social constructivism suggests that only representations of reality are social constructs (e.g. nation); the 'strong' version maintains that the concept itself is socially constructed (i.e. nations exist in a particular manner only because humans have conceived them so).

It should be noted that the discussion of technological change, particularly in the TIP literature, is focused on ICTs. The unique character of ICTs as a technology has fascinated postmodernists, and it is interesting to consider this point of view as well when considering the relationships between technology and social change. This view of ICTs and the role they play in communication and information is generally ignored by TIPs, although it has given rise to a considerable amount of work in cultural studies.

ICTs are fascinating because they were developed in a rationalist, positivist environment comprising mainly white male scientists to support the objectives of a military industrial culture (ARPANET). Given this history, it could be believed that they would be the epitome of scientific rationalism if one assumes the SCOT approach. However, ICTs are different from other tools or technologies: they have assumed a life of their own, and developed the existential freedom of a bastard, disowning their heritage and creating a range of new possibilities, and this cannot be easily understood by TD. Poster explains:

> The Internet resists the basic conditions for asking the question of the effects of technology. It installs a new regime of relations between humans and matter and between matter and nonmatter, reconfiguring the relation of technology to culture and thereby undermining the standpoint from within which, in the past, discourses developed ... about the effects of technology. (Poster, 1995)

He continues: 'Put differently, the Internet is more like a social space than a thing so that its effects are more like those of Germany than those of hammers' (Poster, 1995).
Braidotti agrees:

> Approaching the issue of technology in postmodernity consequently requires a shift of perspective ... Far from appearing antithetical to the human organism and set of values, the technological factor must be seen as co-extensive with and intermingled with the human. This mutual imbrication makes it necessary to speak of technology as a material and symbolic apparatus, i.e. a semiotic and social agent among others. (Braidotti, 1994)

The ICTs are a unique multifunctional technology that combines the creation, manipulation, publication, storage, retrieval and communication of information in one transparent and seamless assemblage. In particular, they form a communications phenomenon, facilitated by computers, rather than a computer phenomenon facilitated by tele-communications. Because of their particular technical nature, it is a network that can be defined, built and used by its own community. Anybody can set up a website and provide information, and this ability challenges power and authority, and can be used for subversive and even criminal ends.

TIPs embedded in context

The TIPs do not exist in isolation from social developments, and it is surprising that there has been a great deal of consistency and lack of change in fundamental principles and applications of the information professions for well over a century. Various theories suggest that responding to a changing environment is inevitable, but the nature of the response within the TIPs has largely been the incorporation of systems built elsewhere in an effort to reduce staff numbers within libraries, records management centres and archives. The TIP literature has not generally embraced wider analyses of the influences of ICTs, or referred to literature which does so, particularly in Cultural Studies. This suggests one of the major reasons why TIPs are not central to the IS.

Note

1. 'Intertwingularity is not generally acknowledged – people keep pretending they can make things deeply hierarchical, categorizable and sequential when they can't. Everything is deeply intertwingled' (Ted Nelson). Available online at: *http://en .wikipedia.org/wiki/Intertwingularity*.

5

What is the Information Society anyway?

A much-noted effect of the development of information technologies has been the formation of the Information Society. While the phrase 'the information age' dates back to at least 1903 (Lubar, 1993), defining the IS is still not clearer than the following: '... an ongoing articulation of political, economic and ideological arrangements and relations' (Slack and Fejes, 1987: 1). Its central characteristic is the use of ICTs which pull and transform the viewer into a participant interacting within a total information environment. ICTs are not just about using but about shaping knowledge and culture. This resonates again with Heisenberg's principle of uncertainty, which posits that on the subatomic level the act of observing changes the nature and relationship of the viewed (Capra, 1996).

Whether the determinist, neutral or social shaping theory of the relationship between information and society is adopted, there is no doubt that ICTs changed the ways in which communication takes place in many parts of the world, and as a result the nature and fabric of societies and organisations have altered, predicated as they are upon their information flows. It is understood that the resultant changes in communication and information flows have changed the essential components of society itself. Any sphere in which the communication of information is important – such as economics, education, law, journalism, politics or business – has been affected.

Technotopia?

Lyon (1988) noted that there are two common beliefs about the IS: first, a total social transformation is predicted; and secondly, this transformation is generally seen as progress. Kofler notes that technology is seen as the driver for economic growth (and consequent prosperity) after having examined a number of European policies to implement an IS, as the issue has been given substantial prominence (Kofler, 1998). Rewards for the implementation of an IS are seen to include global competition, job creation, economic growth and general improvement in the quality of life.

Progressive views of the role of ICTs in the formation of the IS have been enunciated at governmental level, where scenarios for the IS are constructed. One early and widely circulated report, *Europe and the Global Information Society*, was produced by a committee chaired by former European Commission Vice-President, Martin Bangemann (1994). The report is written with the heady optimism and excitement that characterised some of the early Clinton-Gore reports about a National Information Infrastructure in the US, and provides an enthusiastic vision of a globally integrated Europe. The Bangemann report emphasises the role of ICTs in a social revolution:

> Information technology can be used as a vehicle to help eliminate social and economic inequities. IT tools and applications can provide opportunities that transcend barriers of race, gender, disability, age income and location. The enabling quality of the technology, in

addition to the cultural values cultivated through its most well known application, the Internet, carry a democratising potential that already has transformed our social interactions and economic opportunities, both at home and abroad. (Bangemann, 1994)

A different type of utopian view was that a new culture could be created online. Cyberculture would be subversive and counter mainstream thought, featuring a mixture of debate, imagination and futurology; it would exhibit a high degree of cooperation, bonhomie and *esprit de corps*, and a lack of external authority, as described by Howard Rheingold in 1993. Feminism was included in the exuberance, with writers such as Sadie Plant (1997) and Donna Haraway (1991) declaring cyberfeminism as the way forward.

Technology or information, anyone?

Castells' analysis is driven by the hypothesis of a new society: 'A new society emerges when and if structural transformation can be observed in the relationships of production, in the relationships of power, and in the relationships of experience' (Castells, 1998: 340). Castells' claim is that our societies are organised around human processes structured by the historically determined relationships of production, power and experience and that ICTs have changed, or have the potential to change, these processes.

He argues that 'two macro trends ... characterize the Information Age: the globalization of economy, technology, and communication; and the parallel affirmation of identity as the source of meaning' (Castells, 1998: 311). Castells identifies a key feature of the IS as 'informationalism'. It is 'informational' because in the economy, higher productivity and success in competition depend on economic actors' ability to utilise information in the process of creating innovations and new information. He draws a distinction between an 'information society' and an 'informational society' based on an 'informational mode of production' which is useful here (Castells, 1989). Instead of distinguishing between an industrial and a post-industrial economy we could better distinguish between two forms of information or knowledge-based industrial, agrarian and service production (Castells, 1997: 20).

The IS appears to have had more to do with the technology than information. Suffice it to say that ICTs, with their offshore multinational manufacture and built-in obsolescence, are similar in many ways to cars or clothing. The ICTs have created a great deal of profit for certain manufacturers.

The role of information itself is in fact is seldom considered. Ekecrantz asks, 'What kind of society is the information society? Is it constituted of a unique set of social structures and relations? Or is it merely a society within which there exists a certain amount of something called information?' (Ekecrantz, in Slack and Fejes, 1987). In the past few years, there has been a decided step away from prioritising technology as the centrepiece of change and therefore also from the 'technology push' approach, Robins and Webster assert that 'nowadays the focus is on information – rather than information and communication technologies – as the key source of change' (Robins and Webster, 1997: 3).

Informatisation is not a purely technological concept, but is used to indicate the penetration of all information activities into all economic sectors and industries. In contrast, the role modern ICTs play in the transformation of society is regarded as a minor one when compared to the major part played by information. Robins and Webster conclude that they are 'unimpressed by the superficial appearance of computers and telecommunications as "technological revolutions" ... We see them, rather, as just the most recent phase in the history of the technological mediation of capitalist social relations' (in Slack and Fejes, 1987: 104–5). Robins and Webster quote Oettinger:

> ... for Anthony Oettinger (1980, 192), 'without information, nothing has meaning ... Every society is an information society and every organization is an information organization, just as every organism is an information organism. Information is necessary to organize and to run everything from a cell to General Motors or the Pentagon'. (Robins and Webster, in Slack and Fejes, 1987)

Castells states that information itself is not seen as key to social transformation:

> What characterises the current technological revolution is not the centrality of knowledge and information, but the application of such knowledge and information to knowledge generation and information processing/communication devices, in a cumulative feedback loop between innovation and the use of innovation. (Castells, 1998: 32)

Innovation is of course also closely related to the development of competitive advantage in a capitalist economy.

In this sense, ICTs appear to support capitalism and encourage only that social change which preserves economic privilege and prevents its overthrow (Schiller, 1989: 106). Pippin explains quite clearly how knowledge and technologies are considered to protect and preserve existing ideologies through creating structures that reinforce power structures.

> First, one may posit as a general theoretical position that any knowledge process, mediated by an existing social structure, will tend to reproduce that structure. Second, theories of science and technology organized in a knowledge process which is selectively biased in favour of class, race or power elites transform theory into ideology. In short, technological innovations have no social meaning for change, progress, or regression in and of themselves; that meaning arises from their use. In a class or other system of privilege, that use is shaped by those who control the technology. Thus, IT, however advanced, if mediated by a class system, will tend to strengthen and preserve ideological class relations. (Pippin, 1995: 121)

There are several indicators which can be used to assess a technology: where does funding for particular projects originate? what artefacts and practices are developed? whose interests do they serve? are the effects positive or negative? Much funding for the development of IT and networking originated in the US military. The objectives of these technologies include the globalisation of capitalism, increased efficiency and increased competitive advantage for big business, while those who benefit are generally English-speaking, healthy, male, white and affluent.

Pippin concludes: 'The depressing answer ... has to be that IT is not developed through democratic discussion based on human wisdom. Rather, IT is a means for economic survival developed by a world capitalist system hit by a serious crisis and struggling desperately to survive ...' (Pippin, 1995: 141).

Social change

The debate on the IS can be systematised according to the dimensions in which social change is exemplified. Kling identifies five genres of commentary on socio-technical developments of our age (technological utopian, technological anti-utopian, social realism, social theory and analytical reduction), and notes that: 'The conventions of each of these genres limit the kinds of ideas which authors can explore and communicate effectively' (Kling, 1994), so none will give us a clear view of the total effects. (It is interesting to note that this comment is applicable to the information professions as well.) Kling ignores, however, the useful convergences between information science, communication theory, philosophy and cultural studies which permit exploration between diverse factors and their influences, and also that there is a significant difference between academic discourse and that of government and business.

Information economy

One aspect of the IS is the notion of an information economy. The relationship between the economy and technology is as strong as that between culture and technology. The phrase 'information economy' refers to a post-industrial world where people use intellectual rather than physical skills and includes the manufacture and exchange of all information goods and services, such as publishing, entertainment, documents and their transmission. The 1997 Australian Information Policy Advisory Council (IPAC) indicated that:

> The information economy is a global society which transcends national borders and within which many activities are location-independent and geographically

neutral. The governing parameter is globalisation; the emergence of institutions which are not primarily defined by their being associated with any particular nation ... Domestic policies must be geared to international, cross-border realities. (Australia, IPAC, 1997)

Developments in ICTs have created a new form of global capitalism, in which information features as a commodity. Mosco observes that: 'Commodification refers to the process of turning use values into exchange values, of transforming products whose value is determined by their ability to meet individual and social needs into products whose value is set by what they can bring in the marketplace' (Mosco, 1996).

Information has ceased to be something which conveys meaning and is now viewed as an object with a financial exchange value in a market economy. Information as a commodity is understood to be the foundation for economic growth and well-being, signifying progress. Information has been regarded as the 'fourth resource', after labour, capital and plant. Information assets have a financial value, and they include data, information and explicit knowledge that are structured, communicable and transferable among human beings. Information, it is believed, can be used to acquire competitive advantage in the marketplace, and is being transformed from the collective and uncontrolled to the private and controlled. Capurro notes:

> The old principle that the acquisition of knowledge is indissociable from the training of minds ... is becoming obsolete and will become ever more so. The relationship of the suppliers and users of knowledge to the knowledge they supply and use is now tending ... to assume the form already taken by the relationship of commodity producers and consumers to the commodities they produce and consume – that is, the form of

value. Knowledge is and will be produced in order to be sold; it is and will be consumed in order to be valorised in a new production: in both cases, the goal is exchange. Knowledge ceases to be an end in itself; it loses its 'use-value'. (Capurro, 1996)

The invention of the technology of printing gave rise to the concept of copyright, first embodied in the Licensing Act of 1662 in the United Kingdom, and soon followed by the 1709 Statute of Anne which passed into law that copyright in books and other writings gained the protection of an Act of Parliament. The purpose of this and subsequent legislation was to preserve the intellectual property rights of an author or creator for economic reasons. In the IS, there has been a considerably shift of emphasis, expressed in the phrase 'intellectual capital', which comprises both human and knowledge capital. Human capital includes the individual skills and knowledge possessed by human beings, while knowledge capital includes patents, manuscripts, reports and other forms of documented information. Intellectual property is regarded as a commercial product.

The recognition of intellectual capital drives the current field of knowledge management (KM), whereby knowledge possessed or recorded by employees can be used as a strategic asset which can be used to provide competitive advantage, thus increasing profits. With this in mind, the 'learning organisation' is encouraged – so that employees can learn more and consequently be more valuable through their increased knowledge.

The economics of information are extraordinarily complicated because of the nature of information itself. Information has characteristics that distinguish it from physical objects and its values exist on a subjective, relative and existential level, never in an absolute sense. Value depends on the use that someone may make of information at a particular moment in time and space. Information cannot be consumed or moved from place to place and, therefore, it cannot be owned in the normal sense. What can be controlled is access to, and subsequent use of, information. This has traditionally been done through the control of physical documents: this is more complex in the digital world.

Fritz Machlup, an economist, specifically examined knowledge and information as commodities within the US economy from the 1960s and produced several seminal works which deal with this topic.[1] The term 'information economy', therefore, better describes an economy where IT goods and services are bought and sold, rather than an economy based on the buying and selling of information itself (Myburgh, 2003). IT produces information artefacts for the market and may assist in transmitting information but does not engage in knowledge transfer.

The distinction between the IS as a society in which technology dominates and a society in which information itself is used for social benefit is a critical one and is not yet fully explored or expressed by the TIPs. The TD view which has been adopted by this professional group concentrates on the accommodation of ICTs into existing structures and philosophy. The changes, latent or patent, to the core of the profession (providing information for use) have not yet been articulated and developed.

Globalisation

The other major feature of the IS and the information economy is globalisation. 'Globalisation' is a term used to describe processes of social change having any kind of international dimension: changing economies, power relations, communication, cultures and organisations. The IS is 'global' because the central functions of production, consumption, communication and other areas of social action are organised on a global scale through global networks. The term is used most commonly to indicate inclusive, transnational economic processes that take place – completely or partially – outside the control of the individual nations, such as through multinational companies. Globalisation is associated with the development and application of ICTs.

Globalisation is a term with multiple ideological and evaluative connotations. As Risager (1999) notes, globalisation is sometimes conceived as an undesirable homogenisation process which leads to increased international competition, as well as undermining the economies and welfare of poorer nations. Globalisation is associated with the establishment of a dominant world-view and as a mechanism for increasing power, profits and homogeneity, specifically western and often North American. Kellner observes that this increases consumerism and the demand for material goods: 'A world market economy disseminates throughout the planet fantasies of happiness through consumption and goods and services that allow entry into the phantasmagoria of consumer capitalism' (Kellner, 1999). Webster describes how power and control can be maintained through ICTs:

> ... it has been the creation of information networks that has allowed decentralisation of many aspects of economic and social organisation to be combined with increased centralisation of decision-making ... centralised groups at headquarters can in fact monitor and co-ordinate highly dispersed (and hence decentralised) organisational interests. Globalised information systems provide corporations with the infrastructure to allow

world-wide decentralisation of operations while ensuring that centralised management remains in overall control. (Webster, 1995: 200)

Globalisation and internationalisation are two separate phenomena. Internationalisation is a process that enables or supports globalisation, and is generally viewed positively. A useful definition of 'internationalisation' is 'the process of integrating an international/intercultural dimension into the work of an institution' (Knight and de Wit, 1995). Internationalisation is an imperative adjunct to the globalisation process, as each nation's economy is becoming less self-contained and more integrated into a globalised business environment. It is an undertaking that involves developing an understanding of how activities are conducted internationally, and developing intercultural competencies, on both individual and organisational levels.

Internationalisation can be interpreted in two ways, as it can be seen as predatory and protectionist, using cultural and technological impositions to achieve competitive advantage. However, internationalisation can also provide the opportunity for organisations to defuse some of the more negative characteristics of globalisation, by demonstrating collaboration, cooperation, solidarity and mutual assistance. This requires some conscious effort, so that a western view of the IPs is not regarded as the norm or the 'best'.

The political economy of the IS

ICTs, the information economy and globalisation can be perceived, as Donna Haraway has put it, as comprising 'the informatics of domination'.[2] Human rights can be threatened through increasing surveillance and invasion of privacy. Communication through ICTs can reinforce the unequal distribution of material and symbolic resources through cost and through the assumption that western capitalist industrialisation is the norm, which becomes a metanarrative which frames these activities.

Theoretically ICTs could build a worldwide network that breaks down the boundaries between countries and removes the cultural barriers between people from different cultures. In reality, this is not the case: access to ICTs is not global or democratic and Internet users are not representative of the world's population. While there are six billion people on the planet, not even one billion have regular access to the Internet, and are not likely to in their lifetimes. Globalisation is partial and elitist.

This denies the view that ICTs can be liberating and democratising as they are not 'progressive' within themselves. Nonetheless, the increased mobility, affordability and even access to information now offered by ICTs have created great interest in the formation of a 'civil' IS, as expressed by the World Summit on the Information Society (WSIS), sponsored by the International Telecommunications Union of the United Nations, which held its first international meeting in Geneva in December 2003. The objective of WSIS is to establish the foundations of an IS for all. Its manifesto reads:

> The digital revolution, fired by the engines of Information and Communication Technologies, has fundamentally changed the way people think, behave, communicate, work and earn their livelihood. It has forged new ways to create knowledge, educate people and disseminate information. It has restructured the way the world conducts economic and business practices, runs governments and engages politically. It has provided for the speedy delivery of humanitarian aid

and healthcare, and a new vision for environmental protection. It has even created new avenues for entertainment and leisure. As access to information and knowledge is a prerequisite to achieving the Millennium Development Goals – or MDGs – it has the capacity to improve living standards for millions of people around the world. Moreover, better communication between peoples helps resolve conflicts and attain world peace.

In spite of the undertone of TD and a considerable amount of optimism, the Civil Society component of the WSIS – which includes educational institutions, non-government organisations, charities and other such diverse non-affiliated bodies – recognises that humans are at the heart of all societies, and it seeks to establish social, political and economic justice in environmentally sustainable ways. The information conveyed by ICTs, and its applications and use, are seen as more important, and ICTs become the means and not the end. The alternative is increasing digital divides.

Frohmann has amusingly noted that, with regard to the political role of information:

> If, as Andrew Ross claims, 'a code of intellectual activism which is not grounded in the vernacular of information technology and the discourses and images of popular, commercial culture will have as much leverage over the new nomination of modern social movements as the spells of medieval witches or consultations of the I Ching' (Ross, 1989, 212–213), then the question of what intellectual activism in information science would look like cannot avoid confronting postmodernist debates about the relationship between the new communication and information technologies and human subjectivity. (Frohmann, 2000)

His remarks suggest closer engagement of IPs with all constituencies. The TIPs have engaged only peripherally with such politicised endeavours and have largely adopted a passive approach, which locates them as spectators rather than activists. The preservation and conservation of cultural heritage (which may be elitist) is being emphasised as the library's position; the role of information itself in education, health, gender issues, democracy and the like is being ignored by TIPs.

Other, non-technological changes

During the past five decades or so, there have been an enormous number of changes in how people live and how societies are organised and operate. It is useful at this point to summarise some of the effects of these changes on the management of information, including changes brought about by technological developments as well as those inspired by other forces.

Postmodernism has highlighted the political nature of information work, which includes libraries, records management and archives. Foucault's description of power/knowledge is particularly relevant here, and an understanding of the political economy of knowledge production is essential to information managers. This includes understanding the distinction that is made between the positivist view of the NS, privileged and disprivileged knowledges (as identified by Derrida), and the inclusion of relative, unmeasurable, intuitive, spiritual knowledges rather than sole reliance on physical, tangible, measurable, empirical, deductive and quantitative modes of knowledge creation. Postmodernism also emphasises the importance of multidisciplinary studies.

Day (1996) has attempted to bring postmodernism to the information profession. He notes that the epistemology of knowledge includes theory, method and object, and that postmodernism allows these to be understood in 'mobile and shifting economies of information flows that allow objects to express themselves in their relations with theories, methods and other objects' (Day, 1996: 319). He argues that since the relation of method to information has always been of interest to librarians, postmodernism pulls education for the IPs from the margins of science to its centre through the study of information. The creation of knowledge is at the heart of all disciplines, as noted, and in this regard, information management should not be seen to operate only in the sphere of HSS, even though it may itself be a social science.

Tuominen and Savolainen (2002) examined the use of information in the light of social constructionism, identifying the social constructs within which users exist. The social constructionist approach can be used to analyse the use of ICTs within the discipline, as well as how knowledge can be socially constructed. Budd and Raber (1996) suggest that discourse analysis, a methodological technique used in postmodernism, can be used in the study of information, and in the analysis of discursive constructions in the literature of information management. Discourse analysis can also be a useful tool in discussions of information that take place outside of the disciplinary literature.

A critical and informed stance should be adopted with regard to technology. While it has been emphasised that technological issues are separate from information issues, such issues go beyond keeping up with technological development and obsolescence. Because of the increasing convergence and transparency of ICTs, the study of information cannot be fully divorced from the study of technology, in particular with regard to its exploitation and use.

Globalisation is a phenomenon that preceded ICTs, although they have played an important role in facilitating it. In the mid-1960s, because of the development of systems theory, it was acknowledged that our planet is one, delicately balanced, ecosystem, rather than a collection of nations whose actions are irrelevant to others. The inter-relationship between systems and subsystems has permeated through a number of disciplines, and created the new concept of environmental understanding known as ecology.

Globalisation, supported by ICTs, ensures that information can be made available internationally, in spite of the digital divides. This should not have the result, however, of strengthening only one (legitimised or endorsed) point of view, and IPs have the responsibility of ensuring and protecting the rights of access of all to all information, in all its diversity and contradiction, in spite of potential danger to the profession.

Lyotard, in his book *La condition postmoderne* (1979), describes the effects of IT on knowledge and its control. He maintains that the ICTs can distort the hierarchical concept of knowledge and weaken its monopolistic control through social groups, such as professions or universities. This increases the possibility of multiple views and dissent. IPs could adopt an international view of the creation of knowledge, including indigenous knowledges, and bodies of knowledge in languages other than their own. IPs can therefore balance the negative effects of globalisation.

Thus far, there has been passive and uncritical acceptance of the growing commercialisation of information. Some have considered that the information professions must accept that they are no longer solely service professions, and should become part of an entrepreneurial market economy, particularly through the provision of social capital. Such commodification is likely to further distort views of how to value information and knowledge.

The IPs also need to recognise their international responsibilities in another regard as well. Information management goes beyond local concerns, particularly in the area of corporate information management in multinational companies. There must be an awareness of cross-domain information flows, and that the boundaries between personal, work group, enterprise and national communications are blurring. The specific implications for information managers include issues such as differences in climate, language, legislation and knowledge of local events and customs, as well as attention to issues of access to information, competitive intelligence, privacy, security and intellectual property.

Professional qualifications need to be internationally recognised because of the increased mobility of individuals, and the parameters of professional accreditation will need to change concomitantly. Universities should recognise that they are no longer educating professionals for a homogenous domestic market any more, particularly with the range of opportunities now available for international educational experiences, including online delivery. The content of programmes should also be internationalised, providing an international view of the profession.

There have been other societal changes during the past five decades as well, as there is seldom only one single cause for change, or a cause for change that has a single effect. Indeed, Foucault rejects the notion that there is any principle that determines the nature of society. Some of the more general changes have been a different understanding of what constitutes literacy, which now includes media, network and technological literacies, besides reading and writing. The form of education is changing from a teacher-based to a resource-based view. Because of ICTs, many now have higher expectations of being able to find and use information. More transparency and accountability is demanded of governments and organisations; at the same time, there is increasing alarm over surveillance, invasion of privacy and protection of national security. There have also been major changes in political definitions, AIDS, the role of terrorists, increased awareness of the fragile ecology of the earth and many others.

This overview of shifts and transformations in society, as well as how to interpret and understand them, demands a new approach to information management, which expands and unifies the field. This should provide the impetus for information professionals to contribute in a more substantive way to social and organisational targets.

Notes

1. These include the three-volume work, *Knowledge: Its Creation, Distribution and Economic Significance* (1980–84); and *The Study of Information*, with Una Mansfield (1983).
2. A most useful collection of papers has been gathered in an e-book edited by Bousquet and Wills (2004), entitled *The Politics of Information*. Available online at: *http://www.altx.com/ebooks/infopol.html*.

6

A Kuhnian paradigm shift, perhaps

It's on the way

It is argued here that not only is a paradigm shift necessary, but there are already indications that it is occurring. According to Kuhn (1962), a paradigm shift entails not only a change in theory, but a change in the entire world view of those involved. The outline of Kuhn's model is well-known. In brief, Kuhn argues that scientific activity is characterised by paradigms; these 'disciplinary matrices' or world views provide scientists with scientific norms and values, orientations toward phenomena, rules to identify which problems are important and which trivial, and methodological exemplars upon which to model efforts of enquiry. Over time, anomalies accrue within a disciplinary matrix, and these either cannot be solved by the dominant paradigm, or even contradict its basic tenets. A crisis occurs when there are a number of anomalies, and a different paradigm is formulated.

Foucault appears to concur with this phenomenon. He notes that

> ... discourses of life, labor and language were structured into disciplines; how in this manner they achieved a high degree of internal autonomy and coherence, and how these disciplines ... changed abruptly at several

junctures, displaying a conceptual discontinuity from the disciplines that had immediately preceded them. (Foucault, 1984)

It is of course difficult to argue for a paradigm shift in the IPs, as the previous exploration has indicated that either the field has no paradigm, or is multiparadigmatic. Nonetheless, a number of anomalies can be identified, which indicate a necessity for investigation in this area.

Anomalies

Anomaly 1: The IPs do not manage information and neither do they explore the role of information in society. This results in confusion concerning the aims and objectives of the IPs.

The IPs have been preoccupied with documents – Popper's World 3.[1] John Perry Barlow[2] compared information to fine wine: 'We thought for many years that we were in the wine business. In fact, we were in the bottling business. And we don't know a damned thing about wine' (Barlow, 1994). A result of this is the IPs have not devoted enough attention to World 1 (the world as it exists) and World 2 (the world as it has meaning for us) in order to support the professions. An information perspective locates users, technology and information professionals within a socially constructed, complex context.

Considering the meaning of the content of a document and how it might be interpreted lends a new dimension to information work which has not been explored. Provision of information typically does not go beyond the mere provision of a document, or even a reference to it. The emphasis on documents has led to the identification of the professions with place.

Closely aligned with the lack of emphasis on information is the lack of understanding of its role in organisations and society. The link between information management and its societal role is made, for example, by Van House:

> To focus too closely on the institution of the library in which librarianship has largely been practiced is to miss the social problems that it addresses and the fact that the tools, methods and values that define librarianship will continue to do so as its institutional base changes. For our profession to compete successfully, it must identify and assert its professional niche on the larger societal stage. (Van House, 1996)

Document management developed even before formal systems of writing, in the form of bead patterns or marks upon wood. Warehouses of documents have been established ever since it was possible to record information, and became differentiated over time according to the primary purposes they were to serve. We know that cuneiform tablets were kept in repositories in Sumeria from 3000 BC in Mesopotamia, and in King Ashurbanipal's library in Nineveh around 600 BC, although these were probably records repositories or archives.

All other documents were managed in libraries of various kinds. Various types of libraries evolved over time, defined largely by the objectives of their funding sources, such as private libraries, church libraries, university libraries, school libraries, libraries for private organisations and associations, government libraries and libraries for the public at large – in fact, any identifiable human enterprise requiring ready and constant access to information.

The ethos of libraries, as we currently understand them, was established about 170 years ago, when the first 'free' tax-supported library in the world was established in the

1820s in Cape Town, South Africa, by Lord Charles Somerset, based on a tax imposed on wine barrels. Public libraries have come to be the most numerous and obvious embodiment of the TIPs, while librarianship, in turn, is regarded as the public face of the IPs, so it is worthwhile examining them when attempting to determine the role of IPs, and of information, in society. It is the ethos of the public library in particular which characterises it as a social organisation.

While all major religions have a history of benevolence, there was a revitalisation of this activity in western culture from around 1830, and library development subsequent to this date was in large part due to philanthropists, among whom Andrew Carnegie is prominent. Due to the generosity of this wealthy (self-made) industrialist and his passion to establish free public libraries to make self-education available to everyone, 2,509 public libraries were established between 1903 and 1917 (Carnegie Corporation, 2004). This work was continued by state and local authorities, so that by the mid-1950s, the populations of most developed English speaking nations had access to them.

The concept of a 'university of the poor' gave librarianship (and, by association, archives and museums) the aim of enculturation, embracing education and community development. As a result, public libraries are poorly differentiated from social work agencies, except that they are called upon to deal with 'information problems' rather than any other type of problem.

Any large general library, and indeed even a small corporate library or 'information centre', seeks to fill the impossible task of being all things to all people, the node on the information web through which one can access the world. This has involved libraries in, for example, literacy classes, whereas the proper work of the information professional in this case should probably cease once a sufficient supply of materials suitable for neo-literates has been ensured. Travelling along this path can take the information professional far away from the presumed professional base.

The tenet of providing 'free' (albeit tax-supported) access to documents is considered fundamental to the TIPs, even though it has a very recent place in the history of document management. In addition, it has long been assumed that access to documents (and the information they contained) would provide a demonstrable social good. With such a vague and indefinable purpose, it comes as no surprise that assessment and justification prove equally intangible.

The impact that the Carnegie libraries might have had on their communities is poorly documented, as the problem then, as now, is the lack of indicators for measuring public or social benefit. There has been little examination of precisely what the outcomes are of providing such access: the role of information and its use in society is not problematised. Many libraries now attempt to describe such public benefit as 'social capital', a phrase coined by Jane Jacobs in *The Death and Life of Great American Cities* (1961) in order to indicate those social conditions which unite a community to act against antipathetic business and government.

Bourdieu (1986), also concerned with the rights of minorities and excluded classes, identified three forms of capital: economic, cultural and social. He aligns the concept of capital with that of power, and recognises that there are other potential sources of power than the financial one commonly assumed by economic capital. Bourdieu considers social capital to comprise all actual and potential resources associated with a more or less formal network established through personal contact. Such networks enable even those normally disadvantaged to gain benefits by a distribution of power.

It is interesting to note that this understanding of social capital is strongly linked to the Southern African notion of *ubuntu* and the Chinese concept of *guanxi*[3] – it is not unique to western societies.

Cultural capital is a closely associated idea, which includes non-tangible assets such as social class, academic degrees, family background and even accent, which provide advantage to the possessor. Bourdieu distinguishes between three types of cultural capital: that which is embodied, such as learning undertaken by an individual; that which is objectified, usually represented in cultural artefacts such as books and artworks; and that which is institutionalised, which acknowledges the cultural capital of an individual. Bourdieu suggests that educational institutions serve the purposes of the upper and middle classes by recognising cultural capital, and this system becomes hegemonic by exclusion, reproducing the power system of the social structure (Bourdieu, 1993). It is useful to note that in all cases, cultural capital is linked to economic capital. Bourdieu notes that the different types of capital can be converted to other forms. Culture, therefore, is an asset that can add to wealth.

Putnam has a view of social capital that is rather different. He defines the phrase as 'the collective value of all "social networks" [who people know] and the inclinations that arise from these networks to do things for each other ["norms of reciprocity"]' (Putnam, 2000). While Bourdieu saw cultural capital specifically as an indicator of wealth, Putnam aligns social capital with physical capital, including objects and money, natural capital (natural resources) and human capital (the properties of individuals). He also sees social capital as a basic necessity for democracy.

Ideologically, it is easy to read Putnam as a proponent of western late capitalism and materialism, and a supporter of the maintenance of a power status quo. Democracy is associated both with capitalism and modernity; social capital is clearly associated by Putnam with economic growth – so much so that the notion has now been taken on board by the World Bank as part of their initiative to conquer poverty.

The problem here is twofold: firstly, the development of social capital is seen as a good, but one has the problem of associating economic growth and 'goodness'. Wealth is not known to be a predictor of happiness, except perhaps for the very poor; other aspects of experience contribute more substantially to a feeling of well-being. In addition, we can note dissatisfaction on several fronts with contemporary western capitalism. Among these are consumerism and an emphasis on instant hedonism, profit before most other considerations (such as ecological impact or health), a relativistic system of morality which is confusing, and an emphasis on the individual rather than the community, particularly as families become increasingly fragmented.

While ideologically one might not agree with the above (that Putnam's view of social capital serves western capitalism uncritically), he does emphasise that social capital is good not only because of affective responses, but indicates that there are '... a wide variety of quite specific benefits that flow from the trust, reciprocity, information and cooperation associated with social networks', and that it 'creates value for the people who are connected' (Putnam, 2000). These benefits appear to be difficult to articulate and to measure, as there are multiple variables, such as a decreased crime rate, dropping numbers of suicides or increased health. There are also complex and subtle interactions between them, making measurement difficult and possibly inaccurate. The World Bank recognises key indicators such as trust, civic engagement (participation in community or political activities) and social networks.

Social capital is a multidimensional concept, and there are additional semantic difficulties with terms such as 'community' and 'network' (World Bank, 2004). Due to considerable interest in the concept in Australia, Davis and Hall have reported that the Australian Bureau of Statistics has developed a measurement framework which will be expanded in the 2006 General Social Survey (Davis and Hall, 2004).

The World Bank has identified the sources of social capital as families, communities, firms, civil society, the public sector, ethnicity and gender (anything that links people together) (World Bank, 2004). Other groupings, such as gangs or terrorist groups, may exhibit similar characteristics but effectively detract from social capital – the results of social capital development may be subversive or negative. Libraries and archives can also be subversive sites (they are not listed by the World Bank as sources of social capital) by providing access to a range of alternative points of view. A little knowledge may be a dangerous thing ...

A primary problem for the TIPs is identifying social capital as an outcome of information management activities. The role of information and libraries in society is not mentioned in this particular body of literature; there is little analysis of the role of information in such networks and how it can indeed contribute to social upliftment.

It is possibly because Putnam states that information flows depend on social capital (although interestingly, he does not make the reverse assumption) that libraries generally, and public libraries in particular, have investigated the topic. It is therefore fascinating to note that Putnam dates the start of the decline of social capital in America from around 1952, by which time public libraries were well-established and freely available in America.

As political sites, document centres may challenge power structures. Access to information has notoriously been blocked in dictatorial and oppressive regimes for fear of quite the opposite of 'public benefit'. In a more surreptitious way, document centres appear quite ingenuously to support a status quo of middle-class values through selection processes. Noddy and Harry Potter are but two of the many victims of this covert form of censorship.

By and large, the ideology of the TIP paradigm is conservative. A reflexive critique of TIP praxis and constructions of access, document organisation, information, information users and information needs grant considerable power to the TIPs to control information flows and support hegemonies.

Besides this, by far the most frequent de facto use of public libraries is for entertainment, in which area they are challenged by a plethora of cheap and easily accessible alternatives. Providing access to documents to keep a population amused has limited importance. This has no doubt contributed to the public library system's struggle for survival.

The IS is not necessarily an informed society. Technology alone is not the answer. What is needed is the information that is communicated by such technologies. The revolution is more about how we use information and understand the world than it is about technology.

Anomaly 2: Information work is considered a social science and its praxis is located substantially in HSS. Ironically, the areas in which there has for decades been exponential increase in the growth of knowledge and documents – the NS – have for the most part had their information handled by IT.

Information work is widely regarded as a social science. TIPs deal with language, psychology, meaning, knowledge and people besides documents, which makes this classification reasonably clear. The position of the information management department in a university is often a contentious issue: for decades, its location has been within Arts, Humanities, Social Science or Education faculties.

IPs should be concerned with the production and management of all information, and understand the creation of all disciplinary knowledges. The assumption is made – and it is often true – that the IPs do not understand scientific processes, and their role in managing information at large, outside of HSS, is not well articulated.

Anomaly 3: Scientific tradition in information retrieval.

Having said this, the largely artificial association of the IPs with 'science' is flawed: the information discipline is not a natural science because of the reliance on exclusively human capabilities. The attempt to follow a scientific model is seen clearly in the area of information retrieval (IR), where there has been much 'borrowing' of concepts, techniques and terminology between the various groups such as computer scientists and information system analysts. Nonetheless, there is no unifying frame of reference. As far as different paradigms are concerned, it has been noted that researchers seem to work exclusively within one paradigm or the other, and mostly ignore the work of those working from a different perspective.

While the Cranfield tests created an archetypal research methodology, in the late 1970s and early 1980s a major paradigm shift placed information use as the focus of the research being conducted. Dervin and Nilan (1986) describe the early phases of this shift in their discussion of Dervin's theory of 'sense-making' and Belkin's theory of 'anomalous states of knowledge (ASK)' (Belkin, 1980). This shift can be described in the following dimensions:

- objective vs. subjective information;
- mechanistic, passive vs. constructivist, active users;
- trans-situationality vs. situationality;
- atomistic vs. holistic views of experience;
- external behaviour vs. internal cognition;
- chaotic vs. systematic individuality;
- quantitative vs. qualitative research.

These models represent conceptual and methodological revolutions: a shift from quasi-scientific and quantitative techniques which focused on the success of systems, indexing languages and searches, to qualitative methodologies which include cultural, sociological and psychological examination of the interaction between systems and users.

IR is central to IP work. It is interesting that this shift has occurred here, but has not as yet penetrated other areas.

Anomaly 4: The IP view of the organisation of knowledge is document-related and hegemonic.

A substantial component of what is considered library theory is the development of classification systems. One of the earliest, and most widely used, is DDC. While it was developed as a system for organising the records of knowledge – books and other media – in physical space in a library, it is nonetheless indicative of a certain way of thinking.

A reflexive critique of classification schemes might indicate relationships between the way in which documents are ordered and expressions of underlying assumptions and systems of social and cultural hegemonies. Various representations of the real world exist in certain relationships with one another, and this can be viewed as reflecting a given structure of reality. There are, however, other classification schemes, such as enumerative, hierarchical, synthetic and analytico-synthetic systems. These are more accommodating and flexible, and ironically more easily manipulated by computerised systems.

An example is the faceted classification scheme developed by Ranganathan, an Indian mathematician and librarian. This system provides a sophisticated method of post-coordinate indexing for the computerised environment. In his model, information has many dimensions and perspectives, each of which can exist in a different relationship with others, or not at all. The scheme allows for each facet to be isolated, and its relationship to other facets described. This helps explain the difference between, for example, the 'blind Venetian' and the 'Venetian blind'. This system destabilises traditional representations of reality or disciplines and allows an infinite number of fluid reconstructions which can reflect the growth of knowledge.

Anomaly 5: Access is not enough.

This anomaly is related to the comment that the IS is not necessarily an informed society. Access to information – or documents – is not enough to achieve the aims and objectives of the TIPs. There are two sides to this: firstly, does reading an entire encyclopaedia result in an educated person who is easily able to make the correct decisions and choices?

Secondly, the assumption that information-seeking only occurs once an individual has entered a warehouse of documents is fallacious. There are many steps between the identification of an information problem and its solution. An individual has to recognise first of all that the problem experienced could be solved by using suitable information, as only after this will the source of such information be considered. It is not uncommon to search for information initially among documents or people who are at hand or available without too much trouble by using the telephone or Internet. It is probably only after these resources have been found inadequate or inaccurate that a trip to the library, archives or records centre is undertaken – and then only if gaining the information is believed to be important enough to warrant this effort.

After this encounter with IPs and documents, the individual's interpretation of the information, its meaning and the sense that it makes is what will ultimately solve the problem or not, and not simply the information contained in the document. A full understanding of human information behaviour, in all its variety, has been strangely lacking in IP theory until very recently (e.g. Allen, 1996; Capurro, 2000; Dervin, 1983, 1992; Julien and Duggan, 2000; Kuhlthau, 1991; McKechnie, Pettigrew and Joyce, 2001; Nahl, 1996; Palmquist and Kim, 1998; Rosenbaum, 1993; Sonnenwald, 1999).

Without understanding the point at which an IP is necessary as intervenor or mediator, it is difficult to assess the IP role or results of IP actions.

Anomaly 6: Increased fragmentation between and among the IPs leads to misunderstanding of their role.

In efforts to overcome the challenges that face the TIPs, the field has become increasingly fragmented but not specialised. On the contrary, it has become diffuse and marred by obfuscation. As a result, information professionals are seen as an unnecessary extra – in organisations there is a belief their role can be taken over by IT or unskilled workers; in society at large, the role they play is questioned, and they are seen as a superfluous cost. It is ironic, for example, that public libraries in South Africa post-1994 have reached a stage of near collapse: one would imagine that they would be considered vital to the establishment and maintenance of an educated free democracy, although this might have occurred because of their previous association with a western middle-class value system.

Anomaly 7: Model of education for the IPs.

A traditional paradigm has been supported in education for these professions. Dewey decided on four basic subjects when he set up his library training programme, which have remained at the core of the curriculum for more than a century: collection development, bibliographic control, reference sources and services, and administration (whatever they may currently be called). Regardless of social change, different social expectations and changing technologies, a typical education in librarianship, library and information science or library and information studies concentrates on the following areas, even though terminology might vary.

- *Cataloguing and classification.* Even though this may sometimes be called 'organisation of knowledge', little attention is paid to the creation and construction of knowledge, basic epistemology, taxonomy or ontology. Instruction usually includes the use of standardised codes.

- *Reference work.* A brief analysis of the reference interview is followed by an introduction to how to use standard reference works – dictionaries, biographies, bibliographies, abstracts and the like. There is little examination of human information behaviour.

- *Information retrieval.* This mostly revolves around Boolean searching on databases such as that provided by Dialog, and more recently using search engines on the Internet.

- *Management of information institutions.* Such courses normally constitute an introduction to management of staff and organisations in general.

In addition, there is currently an extremely wide array of single courses which attempt to address contemporary needs. These might include records management, information ethics, knowledge management, information literacy, children's literature or multimedia design, but the connection among these strands, and with the core courses, is recondite and even tenuous. TIP education does not reflect the dramatic change in the types of information work available and the potential of the TIP knowledge base in a wide variety of arenas. Much TIP education is, in practice, skewed towards large general libraries, notably public and academic. Instead of receiving a core education which can be interpreted and applied across a wide range of information work, students have been led to believe that other areas of information work are deviant exceptions.

Graduates emerge from such programmes with little or no knowledge of information or users, arguably the most important areas for information professionals. This might suffice if we accept Taylor's (1972) definition of a library as 'a social institution, or combination of institutions, which will raise the probability of effective use of data, information, knowledge and artistic form in all media in support of education (both formal and serendipitous), leisure enjoyment, research and decision-making.' But there is even, rather surprisingly, little work on ethnographic studies of reading, literacy studies or the effects of the print culture.

Butler, in 1933, felt that the important components of LIS were, as Buckland notes, '... statistical methodology, the psychology of reading, the history of the book, the history of the library as an institution, the history of knowledge, and bibliographic history. There is also some discussion of the principles of collection development' (Buckland, 1996). The breadth and theoretical bias of these choices is interesting.

It is difficult to imagine that the first professional qualification of the kind generally offered to TIPs can be a useful basis for the variety of information work that now needs to be done. This effectively weakens the professional domain, as skills are seen as limited and focused, rather than diverse, multidimensional and applicable to a wide variety of situations.

Can these anomalies survive?

TIPs have shown, through the embodiment of their professions in collections of selected and managed documents, a long-standing leitmotif of provision of access to documents on a socially and institutionally cooperative and non-profit basis. There is scant recognition among the TIPs that the kind of work traditionally performed by those dealing with groups of published documents such as journals and books (covered by national and international standardisation, legislation and bibliographic control mechanisms) is different in kind and degree from the work required in a hypertext, networked, digital environment; the work required in a physical institution like a library, records centre or archive is different from that required for managing virtual information flows in intelligent, learning, networked organisations.

The TIPs are important, and many will continue to survive. Libraries, archives and records centres have many functions which guarantee their continuing role as social institutions. As shared resources, they encourage a sense of community and civic pride; they can provide a wide range of viewpoints necessary for an informed democracy and for independent creative thought; they preserve culture.

Professional prospects are driven by the needs of organisations and society, and the range of information work is much bigger and more diversified than many realise. In

2001, Myburgh completed a longitudinal study of job advertisements for information professionals over the previous five years in which the competencies and knowledge base for each job were analysed. This report and its conclusions appear as the Appendix to this book.

The TIPs can be described as simulacra, in that they do not really exist as information professions and only appear to be doing so by the use of words. This means that they are not strong enough to withstand the forces of change and to challenge existing power structures; they have not clarified what they can do to assist survival in the IS; and they have not fully engaged with the complex notion of information management.

There is an urgent sense that some repositioning is necessary for those involved in this most ancient and modern of professions which is both peripheral (too book-based?) and central (TIPs do deal in information, after all) to the IS. Van House, among others, has noted that 'Within the library and information studies (LIS) community, a broad consensus has emerged that the information world is undergoing fundamental change, and that both the LIS profession and education for LIS must respond' (Van House, 1996).

Most theorists consider challenging the assumptions of an embedded power group to be the key responsibility of the power group itself. Here we can agree with Jerry Garcia of the Grateful Dead, who stated, 'Somebody has to do something, and it's just incredibly pathetic that it has to be us'.

Notes

1. Popper distinguished between three worlds:

> By 'world 1' I mean what is usually called the world of physics, of rocks, and trees and physical fields of forces. By

'world 2' I mean the psychological world, the world of feelings of fear and of hope, of dispositions to act, and of all kinds of subjective experiences.

By 'world 3' I mean the world of the products of the human mind. Although I include works of art in world 3 and also ethical values and social institutions (and this, one might say, societies), I shall confine myself largely to the world of scientific libraries, to books, to scientific problems, and to theories, including mistaken theories. (Popper, 1973)

2. John Perry Barlow is a retired Wyoming cattle rancher, a former lyricist for the Grateful Dead, and co-founder of the Electronic Frontier Foundation. Since May of 1998, he has been a Fellow at Harvard Law School's Berkman Center for Internet and Society.

3. These concepts have to do with value systems, kindness and interest in others, and acting for the common good. Mandela has described it as being human only through the humanity of other human beings. It is easy to see how such approaches can assist in supporting the very poorest communities.

7

The IP mosaic

Distinguishing between the information professions

The fragmentation of the IPs might be considered a sign of maturity and growth, but, on the other hand, among small groups of professionals in the same domain performing similar work the effects are mostly negative, leading to rivalry, repetition, duplication and ultimately misunderstanding. As Galvin has indicated, divergence between the IPs confuses employers and the public as to what information professionals do; secondly, specialisations and a variety of different academic and professional credentials serve to narrow and limit career options and job mobility for information professionals themselves (Galvin, 1995).

Divergence and overspecialisation can both have negative effects. Within areas such as archives, Cook believes that there is a potential schism between the various specialisations of archivists, as some associate with record-keepers and others with historians and the librarians who work with manuscripts (Cook, 2000b). Cox is of the view that there is already too much of a split between archivists and record-keepers, and adds, 'I believe that this is true on a grander scale, and should include adjacent professions as well' (Cox, 1996), although he is refering specifically to electronic document management. There are differences even within the IPs: documentalists and information scientists see themselves as separate and superior to librarians, who are considered old-fashioned, while manuscript archivists view themselves as different from record-keepers who handle current business records.

Criteria of distinction

- *Place.* Historically, these professions have been separated by the notion of 'place' (a notion, incidentally, that changes the digital world), in particular the institutions in which IPs work.

- *Professional associations.* IPs are separated by different professional associations which have fostered independent traditions which maintain sectoral differences between these groups. A variety of different journals and conferences sponsored by such associations makes it difficult, if not impossible, for an individual to maintain awareness across a number of different areas.

- *User-centred versus system-centred models.* Downie (1999) describes the dichotomy between the user-centred and the system-centred models, the one qualitative and female, the other quantitative and male. Abbott finds that, historically, there have been two general types of information professionals: those who work with qualitative information (an area generally occupied by librarians) and those who work with quantitative information (the domain of cost accountants, management engineers, statisticians, operations researchers, systems analysts and others) (Abbott, 1998).

- *Types of information.* Very frequently, what is meant by this is different types of document, although it can indicate different subject or discipline areas. However, there are also differences such as age; in addition, distinctions can be made between types of information such as statistical, business intelligence, news, scientific research and so on, so, to a certain extent, TIPs are differentiated by the content of the documents they manage.

- *Differences in form.* The IPs are clearly distinguished by the form of the documents they deal with: published or unpublished, monographs, serials, manuscripts, artefacts, legal documents, business forms and so on. Danner (1998) adds that further distinctions can be made between the documents themselves and the means of their communication (which is largely, according to him, the domain of technologists, who are also described as information professionals), which provides a good example of the lack of clarity about what information work comprises. The ways in which the various types of documents need to be managed also indicates differences among the ranks of professionals, even though a certain type of document is not managed exclusively by one particular professional group.

- *Client groups.* The TIPs are distinguished by their client groups, and this applies within these professions as much as between them. Librarians are differentiated according to libraries set up to serve different client groups, such as school libraries, research libraries, public libraries and so on. Some record-keepers are primarily concerned with legal compliance (business), while for others the emphasis might be on preservation of documents. Archivists may work for large organisations like national archives, or smaller individual organisations such as a church.

- *Different technologies.* There are few fundamental differences between the technologies that are used in each of the TIPs, although their particular tools might differ.

- *Different societal roles.* Professions are distinguished by the social need that they respond to, and it is true to say that each of the IPs has addressed a specific range of social and organisational needs: libraries have the overall aim of providing information for education and enculturation; records managers strive to ensure the legitimacy of the records which document the transactions of the organisations for which they work; and archivists have a responsibility to preserve social memory. These are expressed in differences in organisational roles, discipline-specific languages and historically distinct domains of information content.

- *Standards, methodologies and intellectual foundation.* This is probably the most important area to be explored, but remains the least developed area of convergence (because of the elements cited above). It is argued here that all IPs share a similar intellectual foundation, even though this is not clearly articulated. There is limited cross-pollination and multidisciplinary endeavour between the IPs. This has led to the emergence of a plethora of differing, but often overlapping, standards, as well as modes of practice and research topics and methodologies.

However, as Rayward states, 'Over the past 20 or 30 years ... there has been growing awareness that what has been accepted as separating these professions may no longer be relevant and may have become dysfunctional' (Rayward, 1994: 163). Increased cross-disciplinary work is necessary for a variety of reasons, not least to accommodate social and technological change. This can only occur if a common intellectual foundation is recognised.

Points of convergence

While divergence and differentiation exist, there are simultaneously a number of points of convergence. These are ironically reflected most frequently in a commonality of praxis rather than theory, even though each area requires specialised skills. The abstraction of shared principles enables a clearer focus on similarities and differences in praxis across the IPs. All information professionals are engaged with users, information technologies, organisations, information products and services. As a result, in broad terms their tasks and functions are very similar:

- alignment of provision of information with the goals and objectives of the organisation or individual;

- understanding how individual members of such organisations, or sectors of society, might search for information of use to them;

- identifying information and documents that might be used (this might involve asking people who have particular knowledge to record this information in documents);

- collecting documents – whether physically or virtually (through links or databases);

- ensuring the integrity and value of documents;

- describing documents in order to organise them physically or virtually, and to establish the links between them;

- providing access to documents – whether physically or virtually;

- preventing access to documents – whether physically or virtually;

- providing intellectual access to information contained in documents;

- preventing intellectual access to information contained in documents;
- preserving documents – whether physically or virtually;
- discarding documents that have no continuing value;
- discerning, describing, arranging and protecting documents that have exceptional qualities and perceived long-term values.

Shared areas of concern that emerge from these tasks include metadata and thesaurus development, information retrieval, electronic media management, professional ethics, digital document management and preservation, organisational management, database structure and use, organisation of and access to information, evaluation of information, systems analysis, user needs and behaviour, information resources, and laws governing privacy, intellectual property and freedom of information (FOI), among others.

Many express the view that ICTs are the major reason for convergence among the IPs. ICTs themselves have converged and continue to do so (for example, the mobile phone which plays music and takes photographs) and it is logical to presume that divisions would blur between the disciplines that examine them, such as library and information science, records management, archives, psychology, business education, communications, journalism, economics, media, sociology and computer science.

Digital objects are primarily responsible for the erosion of the distinction between those who are custodians of information (librarians and IT specialists are placed in this group) and those who are custodians of artefacts (such as museum curators and archivists), according to Gililand-Swetland (2000). Middleton agrees:

> The apparent convergence of information handling processes engendered by the technology has led to

suggestions of an associated convergence of disciplines. The term 'information professional' itself is an indicator of this process, providing an umbrella for the combination of skills formerly attributed to separate sectors of the workforce. (Middleton, 2002)

Few would deny that the practice of the TIPs has changed over the past decade. Increasingly, these groups (and others) use the phrase 'information professionals' to describe themselves, hoping to indicate that they do something different because of ICTs. The new work is described by job titles that do not use the words 'librarian', 'records manager' or 'archivist'. Examples of these are 'bibliographic database manager', 'document manager', 'business analyst', 'director of electronic learning', 'information manager', 'web coordinator', 'vocabulary resource manager', 'digital preservationist' and 'knowledge network specialist'. Nonetheless, it is still largely the same work, albeit performed by using ICTs as tools. As synonyms go, the change of nomenclature has done little to change the awareness, prestige or image of the professions.

At the higher education level, many programmes in librarianship offer courses or specialisations in archives and records management, even though specialised programmes in these areas also exist (while rare). The blurring of distinctions between records management and archives was well expressed by David Roberts in an e-mail to the Aus-archivists listserv on 21 February 1999:

> [The simple model of the records continuum as defined in the original Australian standard] recognises that records do not magically become something else when we decided that we should keep them as archives – *there is no archival transubstantiation* – and that archives are simply records that we have appraised as having continuing or enduring, as opposed to identifiably

finite, value ... This ... leads inevitably to what is the touchy part of all this: professional turf. If record-keepers and archivists undertake the same processes (an interwoven continuum of such processes) to manage the same things (records) using the same professionally accepted standards..., *why do we want or need two professions?* [Author's emphasis]

Indeed, the same question could be asked across a wider and more inclusive continuum of IPs. Gililand-Swetland (2000), among others, has noted that we might well see a new multidisciplinary metacommunity of information professionals. What will unite them, and support changing practices, is recognition that there are many issues shared by IPs.

Is convergence useful, impossible or inevitable?

There are several reasons why convergence is important. At present, the IPs have little political clout, as they do not present a united front: added to this, there is little clarification of what they can do. There are few senior executive appointments in the existing IPs which allow an integrated and holistic view of information generation, management and use – often senior 'information' appointments are filled by technologists.

Convergence and the establishment of a metacommunity would enable synergies between the IPs, as well as providing a higher profile to each sub-discipline. For individual practitioners, while practice and routines might vary from organisation to organisation, there would nonetheless be opportunities for a much wider range of career paths.

Cohen (1999) has written of the need for a new meta-discipline which he calls 'informing science', which originates largely in the field of information systems. While his focus is essentially large organisations and businesses, he argues that the area of information management is undergoing an evolutionary change, and quotes Turchin (1977), who 'developed the evolutionary construct of Meta-System Transition (MST). An MST occurs when a new control level emerges that integrates a set of subsystems at the level below' (Cohen, 1999). This sounds in some ways similar to Kuhn's description of a paradigm shift.

The historical position of document management allowed for differentiation among the various information professions, as the divisions of place and so on, as mentioned above, made distinctions between them quite clear. Each information profession, in its own right, was a 'meta-system' for a range of specialisations: cataloguing, information retrieval, preservation, systematic bibliography, children's librarianship and the like. However, if the lens is adjusted to focus on information management, the overlap among the professions, in practice and principles, is immediately visible. Managing documents as physical (including virtual) objects becomes a specialisation in itself; the principles of other specialisations, such as cataloguing and information retrieval, are ubiquitous across all information professions, including KM, CI, IA and SIM.

However, what is lacking in the case of the TIPs is identification and description of what this new 'control level' might be, or perhaps, more particularly, what it might be called. It needs to explain common principles in terms of a theoretical infrastructure that is useful and applicable to all aspects of managing information.

A metacommunity cannot merely comprise the 'joining together' of the various areas of information work, even if they share common problems with digital objects. It relies upon a close examination and development of a satisfactory multidisciplinary theory upon which to base information practice, where the diversity of tasks can be recognised and explored. The formation of a metacommunity should not pose a threat to any individual specialisation. If the metacommunity were to consist, for example, of librarians, archivists, technical information specialists, knowledge managers, competitive intelligence officers, information architects, corporate information managers, data managers, information creators and records managers, it must be acknowledged that each of these sub-disciplines owes its distinctive perspective to the recognition of a unique social need. Each sub-profession can be distinguished by its social and organisational role and responsibilities and its praxis, while the underlying theory and knowledge base which support its particular modus operandi would be common to all.

A metaphor might be a table, where the table top represents the unifying theory and each specialisation is a table leg which supports the table top as well as contributing to the overall functioning of the object.

By and large, change has been occurring across the profession by default rather than through any organised or thoughtful development. Responses occur in a piecemeal, even randomised, way as the environment varies and events occur. In 1963, David Braybrooke and Charles Lindblom published a study of policy-making and concluded that the normal method for deciding on policies was that of 'disjointed incrementalism'. Policy change in this mode is incremental in that it is not revolutionary or on a grand scale. Small, or relatively small, problems are involved, and the solutions are prepared and proposed by individuals or by committees. Incremental change seems to be what people can handle most comfortably. Any large change is psychologically threatening, and in any case, the necessary information to predict the consequences of action simply isn't available. The accretion of small changes leads to dissent rather than agreement within the TIPs.

While the accumulation of changes is sometimes overwhelming, this serves as a poor excuse for a fresh and holistic look at where the profession is going. The lack of coherent theory to provide a basis for multidisciplinary intersections and to understand a fundamental shift in the frame of reference complicates responses. A long overdue clarification of what the professions comprise has created a challenge that must be boldly and imaginatively faced. Information professionals cannot be like ostriches, or incremental policy analysts, who 'often rule out of bounds the uninteresting (to them), the remote, the imponderable, the intangible and the poorly understood, no matter how important' (Neill, 1992: 126). What is required is a new disciplinary matrix in order to understand what information work is.

New information paradigm

The trends previously identified posit that people's worlds are constructed through a myriad of social inputs, in an ongoing process in which 'information' (whatever its form) plays a crucial role.

Radford notes that 'Foucault's work has recently been recognised as a potentially fruitful perspective for framing epistemological issues in library and information science' (Radford, 1998), and he has made a most interesting contribution to this debate. Radford suggests that traditional positivist concepts of knowledge, meaning and communication in library and information science are facing a crisis:

they are unable to adequately characterise and structure the experience of interacting with the modern library (or other information institution). He offers 'an alternative postmodern epistemology from which library scholars can rethink traditional notions of the library, librarian and, most importantly, library users' (Radford, 1998).

Such a paradigm should reflect a different world view of the processes of information management. Like the railways not recognising their role in transportation, there has been too much attention paid to documents and to core tasks and competencies, while a broader understanding of knowledge representation, organisation and use has been neglected.

Metatheory for the metacommunity

As Sutton suggests, we may need to 'embrace the inevitable and deliberate obsolescence of extant professional knowledge and skills' (Sutton, 1999), and it would appear that these need to be replaced with a more comprehensive knowledge base which understands information as a universal component of society and its activities.

Interdisciplinarity, transdisciplinarity and multidisciplinarity

Developing a metatheory means designing a new idiosyncratic interdisciplinary speciality of information management. The subject matter must be delimited, and the metatheory requires a specially formulated conceptual and theoretical basis which could suggest research questions and methodologies, and the type and style of result to be aimed at. Bartek has provided a useful argument for the construction of a metatheory, which will resonate with educators and practitioners in the information professions:

> There is too much factual knowledge to grasp even a speck of the whole. This makes for an excessive diversity that lacks in coherent unity. With no coherency in the parts, there will be no coherent truth in the whole. Without coherent truth there is only a relative truth. Relative truth makes for contradiction from different viewpoints, perceptions, and perspectives. Contradictions deny a common definition and meaning of truth, morality, justice, and beauty. They also deny common standards, values, principles, and virtues. Uncommon values lead to personal and social conflict and confusion, to the blocking of learning in education, to the disintegration of social unity. To have common standards and values, that a global theory of knowledge requires, concrete factual knowledge should be unified by abstract concepts that are unified by abstruse principles that are unified by symbolic structures. Such principles ultimately derive from an ultimate unity and structure. This ultimate unity is the keystone that holds the whole systematic structure of knowledge together. (Bartek, 1998)

Theoretical alignment has increasingly become a problem for many researchers, particularly outside of the NS, as it can impose a disciplinary paradigm which might not be helpful. However, this poses particular problems in information management, as this is precisely what is needed, and if it does not exist, it might need to be invented. Information theory cannot be located within any specific discipline, such as communication, mathematics, linguistics, sociology, technology, cultural studies or philosophy. As Foucault has noted, 'Intellectuals have become used to working ... within specific sectors, at the precise points where their own conditions of life situate them' (Foucault, 1984: 68) and obediently adopting the world views and methodologies developed in these disciplines will not solve the present predicament. Disciplinary boundaries can be permeable, however, as adherents of one discipline may in some cases defer to the cognitive authority of another discipline, and in others borrow concepts and conceptual resources when those of their own are insufficient. This would appear to be a useful approach.

Because of the nature of information, an information metatheory would need to incorporate fragments of many disciplines, as well as from specialisations within the field itself, but would draw primarily on information retrieval and information-seeking behaviour, communication and cultural studies, sociology, organisational communication and behaviour, linguistics, philosophy, gender studies and social informatics.

It is suggested that knowledge creation and information use are transdisciplinary by nature. Westbrook defines interdisciplinarity as 'the purposeful weaving together of two or more disciplines that are usually considered to be quite unconnected in order to reach a new understanding, create a new academic end product, or advance research on a particular question' (Westbrook, 1999: 26). Gibbons et al. (1994) have noted that Mode 2 knowledge production is 'transdisciplinary' in that it contributes theoretical structures, research methods and modes of practice that are not located on current disciplinary or interdisciplinary maps. One of its effects is to replace or reform established institutions, practices and policies, which is perhaps a desirable outcome in this case.

Transdisciplinarity can also involve 'borrowing' methodologies from other fields, even if content is not adopted, in order to understand particular problems. This notion is not new: Hayek commented nearly half a century ago: 'There is scarcely an individual phenomenon or event in society with which we can deal adequately without knowing a great deal of several disciplines . . .' (Hayek, 1956: 464). He maintained that many intellectual, social and practical problems require interdisciplinary approaches.

Interdisciplinarity involves multiple simultaneous processing and connection-making, or seeking the whole, and offers one way of understanding the multiple linkages between subdivisions of knowledge so that various factors and their dimensions that shape understanding of the world can be understood. The need for transdisciplinarity arises from developments in knowledge and culture that are characterised by complexity, hybridity, non-linearity, reflexivity and heterogeneity.

Many complex or practical problems can only be understood by pulling together insights and methodologies from a variety of disciplines; many problems require broad holistic approaches. Research problems themselves are generally not independent and sequential but highly interrelated and simultaneous. It is sometimes necessary to look at the whole, even if it means foregoing full knowledge of all the parts.

Information theory is one of these. IPs have historically drawn on a variety of other theories and disciplines. Hjørland believes that LIS is itself a multidisciplinary professional domain, drawing on many kinds of knowledge (Hjørland, 2000a). In archives, Gililand-Swetland notes that archival science has drawn upon areas such as diplomatics, history, law, textual criticism, management and organisational theory, as well as library science (Gililand-Swetland, 2000). Records management is part of a much larger field, including strategic information management, content management, customer relationship management as well as information management. In spite of the problems with its lack of clear definition, information science includes, according to the American Society of Information Science and Technology (ASIST), information retrieval, computer science and engineering, management science, economics, library and classification science, cognitive science and psychology, communication science, behavioural science and information policy.

As early as 1931, Douglas Waples and his colleagues felt that librarianship was ready for a 'critical, academic approach' and that in order for a scientific study of librarianship to develop, an interdisciplinary focus was necessary, demanding contact with other disciplines. Thompson Klein (1996) has researched this idea in some depth, and indicates that a number of concepts and theories have previously promoted a comprehensive vision that metaphorically encompasses all areas of knowledge. The most prominent among these are general systems theory, cybernetics, structuralism, phenomenology, Marxism and feminism (Thompson Klein, 1996).

In addition, transdisciplinary thinking can represent a primary source of intellectual breakthrough. Kaufer and Carley note that:

> ... authors associated with the most authority and change are not rooted within a single intellectual community. Instead, they are authors on the move, the maverick, the eccentric, the outsider, the intellectual migrant, trained in one community and rising to fame after finding their way to another. (Kaufer and Carley, 1993: 384)

A transdisciplinary approach is compelled by the inability of current theory and knowledge to explain the occurrence of the anomalies in information management. It is therefore necessary to annex multiple areas of research in order to consider the theory-building essential to the IPs. For the purposes of this work, this involves the identification of disparate literatures, rather than capturing all of the complexities involved, to provide a better and more coherent understanding of the factors influencing the construction of a unifying theory for the IPs.

However, the development of a multidisciplinary view has been discouraged by the fragmentation of university structure, which is still based on the Aristotelian view of the structure of knowledge, into institutional frameworks that define disciplinary boundaries. Such structures present almost insurmountable obstacles to the creative approaches that are required in order to solve complex information problems.

A caveat must be issued at this point. Interdisciplinary research is problematic and information overload especially threatening, which can lead to difficulties in synthesising the literature across numerous disciplines. It is therefore beyond the scope of this work to articulate in detail what this metatheory can comprise, therefore only suggestions of areas for inclusion are offered.

In some areas there may be a paucity of information in one domain and a glut in another, creating difficulties in analysing and integrating all into a coherent picture (Wilson, 1994), which emphasises the need for a number of experts from a number of areas to work on this problem. Georg Simmel described the 'typical problematic situation of modern man' as that of 'the feeling of being overwhelmed by this immense quantity of culture, which he can neither inwardly assimilate nor simply reject, since it all belongs potentially to his cultural sphere' (Simmel, 1976: 254), and this is certainly the case for the individual exploring the boundaries of information theory.

8

Core information knowledge

In order to respond to societal, organisational and individual needs for information, rather than documents or data, it goes without saying that the new IPs require a broad-based understanding of knowledge and information. In addition, there are a number of areas which require more specialised knowledge, but here, what all IPs should know is emphasised.

What new IPs need to know

The new mode of knowledge production, Mode 2, proposed by Gibbons et al. (1994), suggests that there is a need for skills and knowledge that have thus far not been developed; in addition, such skills and knowledge need to be both multiple and transferable. The change that is required is that of broadening and deepening IP core knowledge so that the needs of our changing society can be accommodated. It is complicated because information underpins and is associated with all types of knowledges and communication, and a diversity of individuals and communities.

As Abbott indicates, the issue is providing a theoretical base for the work done by the professions rather than the structure of the professions. He suggests that sometimes there is new work and sometimes work becomes obsolete; sometimes professions move in an entirely different direction as the needs of society change (Abbott, 1998). In order for information management to respond to challenges, professional education must include the theoretical principles of information management; the emphasis on the acquisition of particular skills must give way to understanding of the range and scope of the professions, which graduates can draw upon when faced with a particular set of circumstances or problems. In this way, the IPs will be able to provide leadership rather than being handmaidens to technology.

What is core knowledge for an information meta-discipline?

Probably the most debated (and contentious) area in education for the information professions is that of what constitutes 'core' knowledge. By and large, this debate has been inward-looking, and the boundaries of the professions, their adjacencies and similarities with other professions, and their place in contemporary culture and society, are not mentioned. There has been enough discussion about how many angels can dance upon the head of this particular pin, and now it is necessary to look at the construction of the garment as a whole.

The Association for Library and Information Science Education (ALISE) investigated the mission statements of many schools in LIS in the United States, and found consensus that professional education for IPs, particularly in the area of librarianship, is understood to include the cognitive and social aspects of how information and information systems are created, organised, managed, filtered, disseminated, routed, retrieved, accessed, used and evaluated. The KALIPER teams reviewed curricula for the field, and identified six trends in education for LIS. These include:

- information environments and problems so that professionals have a grasp of the 'big picture';

- a multidisciplinary but user-centred approach, although a distinct, core knowledge base remains unknown;

- increasing emphasis on ICTs and how to use them;

- more areas of specialisation (which can be read as increasing fragmentation);

- different education delivery options; and

- a variety of programmes at undergraduate and postgraduate levels (ALISE KALIPER report, 2000; Durrance, 2000).

These trends do not indicate much shift in conceptual ground. The KALIPER teams did not investigate the IPs as a whole (in spite of the mention of specialisation), and education for LIS is used as a paradigm for them all. While it is heartening to note the move towards a broader understanding of the role of information in society and in people's lives, it is nonetheless a view from within the TIP habitus. For example, the 'user-centred' view noted above relates almost entirely to the information-seeking behaviour of individuals in libraries or vis-à-vis information systems rather than information seeking in general.

There are a few glaring omissions here: there is no indication of why such activities are performed or important; there is little distinction between the role of documents and the role of information or information systems; and a closer examination of the related syllabi reveals an emphasis on the practice rather than a deeper understanding of the variety of approaches which can be taken in the performance of these activities. There is also no mention of individual, disciplinary, organisational or societal knowledges or epistemological attitudes to knowledge and information.

The argument for the formation of a metacommunity is predicated upon the recognition of a number of tasks and objectives that the information professions have in common, and it is seemingly straightforward to extrapolate from these to indicate the areas of knowledge which are valuable in terms of supporting such activities. The activities include: identifying information needs; understanding how individuals search for and use information identified as being useful to them; identifying and making accessible the documents which provide such information, by describing the documents; protecting the information, both physically and virtually, and preserving documents (and their information) that are believed to have long-term historical or social value.

These seemingly straightforward activities conceal a complexity of underlying knowledge. Just as a medical doctor must recognise that a sore throat, a headache and a fever may indicate a cold, influenza, glandular fever, measles, anthrax, botulism or rabies, among others, and must understand how to prevent, identify and treat these diseases, the IP must understand the complete role of information: its origin and creation, its form of capture and communication, its range of uses, its effects and the results of its effects. In addition, as a medical doctor will use tools such as scalpels and thermometers, IPs have a range of tools (sometimes other documents) to assist in their work, but these are secondary. It is suggested that all IPs should be able to provide some answers to the following questions.

In order to perform information management activities adequately, new IPs need to know something about the following aspects of information, technology and people.

- How is knowledge created, by whom and why?

- How is information recorded and communicated?

- What are the processes of communication?

- What are the differences between data retrieval, information retrieval and document retrieval?

- What are the various document formats in which information is contained?

- How are documents selected, acquired, identified, maintained and preserved?

- What are the various document types, such as public domain, grey literature, and so on?

- What mechanisms are available for the communication and transmission of information? How do they affect the meaning of information?

- Who are the potential users and non-users of information? Why is this so?

- What information might be of interest to specific groups of users? Why?

- How can information delivery and interpretation be improved and enhanced to these users and non-users?

- How is information used? What are the advantages and disadvantages of having access to information, or not having access to information (in both quality and quantity)?

- How can the information within a document best be represented to ensure its retrieval from masses of other information?

- How can information overload be prevented to improve optimum use of information?

- How can the value of information be discerned? What is the value of the lack of information? Why is this important?

- How do ICTs support or detract from information management?

- What roles does information play in the lives of individuals, in organisations and in society? How can these be changed or modified by information professionals or others?

In order to be able to respond adequately to these questions, and others, some knowledge of the following areas is regarded as essential. It is suggested that further investigation into these would assist in the identification of the scope of an information metatheory.

Creation and structure of knowledge

New IPs need to understand the framework of knowledge and knowledge creation, the way knowledges can be structured and the ways in which such structures and their parts are named. Vickery and Vickery (1987) state that what information professionals need to study is information from generation to exploitation (Vickery and Vickery, 1987). This has been reiterated by Cox, who says that IPs must understand

> ... how information is created, the differences between information sources, the distinctions in how people acquire information and turn it into something meaningful to them and their organizations, and the changing nature of information systems as a reflection of social, economic, political, cultural and other factors. (Cox, 1998)

The cultural, social and disciplinary origin and location of knowledges must be considered, and this includes epistemologies and discourses which influence the formation of bodies of knowledge, which includes the ways in which reality is conceived and how truth is conceptualised. New IPs need an understanding of the cultures of individual academic disciplines and a recognition of their differences in research questions and methodologies. It is also necessary to move beyond formal knowledge systems and embrace indigenous knowledge systems and informal knowledge systems that may have little to do with documents, information systems or warehouses of documents. Consider the transmission of information (of various types) by teenagers using SMS messages, for example, in creating and reinforcing particular subcultures.

Knowing how knowledge and information are created assists in the evaluation of knowledge, as well as the understanding of the potential use of information by individuals inside a particular knowledge culture. Examining how knowledge and information are created and represented enables IPs, as information intermediaries, to interpret information on behalf of individuals in other knowledge cultures. Problems might be similar in a number of cultures, but each might regard different solutions as most useful to them.

For the new IP, qualitative methodologies are particularly important as quantifiable measures of the value of knowledge and information can, at best, only be crude. The evaluation of intangibles is quite different from the assessment of a document, while social effects are, in fact, immeasurable. Einstein is believed to have put up a sign in his office reading: 'Not everything that can be counted, counts; not everything that counts can be counted'. Having said that, the ways in which data have been collected, analysed and presented are as important as why they were collected in the first place.

Other elements need also to be taken into account with regard to understanding how and why information comes about. The prevailing 'publish or perish' syndrome in universities could cause initial or repetitive information to be published. The exposure to information derived from mass media and advertising, of whatever quality, helps shape contemporary culture, and a critical approach to these (who creates this information and why?) is also essential.

The areas which could be included here cover:

- introduction to philosophy: ontology and epistemology discourses, philosophy of knowledge, philosophy of information;
- research methodologies;
- statistical analysis;
- cultural studies.

Knowledge representation

Analysis and categorisation

A primary task of IPs is to enable a match between what the creator of the document intended and the meaning as received by the reader or viewer. This is a fundamental issue in communication studies as well, and interpretation of information becomes particularly difficult over space and time. This match is translated by IPs into an intermediary system language – a classification code or index – which, it is hoped, will match the search statement determined by the user. There is clearly room for error in this translation model.

In the Utopia which Plato describes in his *Republic*, he chooses to ban artists. He reasons that they are frauds. When challenged on this position, he explains that there is an idea or concept of a table, for example, that we as humans possess. This concept is not related to a specific kitchen or antique table, but to the very notion of a table – a raised, hard and level surface with multiple uses. It is, according to Plato, a remove from reality to construct such an item. Each of us has a different idea of the perfect dimensions and appearance of such a thing. The carpenter's effort is only a model of what a table might be. The artist, then, who attempts to copy such an article in paint or marble is therefore offering an idea at yet another remove from reality – the table as seen by the artist. Consider the use of perspective, Van Gogh's colours and Picasso's shapes, which illustrate the differences between how individuals may perceive objects and events.

Acting as intermediaries between information and information users, new IPs are like artists. New IPs need to be able to capture the notion of the content, but must rely on their subjective interpretation of this, which is then summarised and represented by language or numerals. It is only in this way that specific information can be differentiated. This is a two-part process: content or subject analysis, and representation by classification or indexing.

Subject or concept analysis is the first step in deciding what information is contained in a document (or knowledge known by a person). The subjectivity of the subject analysis process is particularly apparent in non-text databases. Consider how a photograph may be interpreted as: 'A family on a picnic next to a river', 'An old-fashioned picture', 'A picture of my grandmother's 30th birthday party', 'The Muddy Creek before canalisation', 'An example of a Model 8 Ford in Australia', or even an example of a particular photographic technique.

Subjectivity is also apparent in information use, which is impossible to predict by an IP. A receipt for 12 kilos of arsenic might provide evidence of a financial transaction or a murder. A tally of jars of olive oil might provide valuable insights into population density and cultural development 40 centuries later. Additionally, we are all familiar with examples of literature which can be read at various levels – *Gulliver's Travels* and *The Little Prince* come to mind.

The attempt is made to reduce the 'aboutness' of a document not only to a sentence ('This book is about...'), but to a few words ('losses', 'live sheep transport', 'Australia', 'Iran'), which summarise the potential (often quite different from actual) ways in which the information might be sought. Subject analysis needs to consider information contextually. For example, the subject of a document about road-building in the Roman Empire might consider the aspects of technology, communication, political strength, history, archaeology or cultural invasion.

Concept analysis is therefore part of subject analysis. It is a technique that links together groups of ideas (which in turn assists in categorising them).

> Concept Analysis uses objects, attributes and conceptual classes as its basic constituents. A *conceptual class* consists of any group of entities or *objects* exhibiting one or more common characteristics, traits or *attributes*. A characteristic is a conceptualized attribute by which classes may be identified and separated into a conceptual hierarchy, and further subdivided (specialized) by the facets of topic, form, location, chronology, etc. (Neuss and Kent, 1995)

In both subject and concept analysis, therefore, is an impetus to group like ideas. The ideas themselves need to be connected, and their relationship within the information of the document must be expressed. Some documents dealing with road-building in the Roman Empire might deal exclusively with inventing concrete; others might deal with the advantages or disadvantages of road-based communications in a far-flung empire.

By grouping like ideas, a process of categorisation is begun, indicating relationships between concepts. Categorisation is a discursively constructed activity. A hierarchical relationship of concepts has long been a tradition in western thought, from Aristotle to Melvil Dewey. This denies the simultaneous existences of objects (and even concepts): a potato can be considered as a cooking ingredient, a source of particular nutrients or poisons, an agricultural product, the preferred food of certain insect pests or even a subject for a poem.

Potter explains that the NS, where the physical world is dealt with, is quite straightforward in comparison with the HSS.

> In realist discourse, where language is the mirror of nature, categorization is understood as a rather banal naming process; the right word is assigned to the thing that has the appropriate properties. In contrast, in the discourse of the construction yarn that I have been elaborating, categorization is much more consequential. It is through categorization that the specific sense of something is constituted. (Potter, 1996: 177)

An ontology represents a specifying scheme of concepts which holistically describes some topic. It can be compared to a formal vocabulary or index, and includes logical descriptions of the items, relationships between items and how items cannot be related. Categorisation, by indicating relationships, is not a neutral activity but, in Potter's view, should be understood as influential ways of producing forms of knowing that meet the rhetorical standards of the communities of speakers in which they will be shared (Potter, 1996).

Physical representation of documents

The representation and organisation of information and information resources is a primary focus of the IPs, and when all documents enjoyed physicality, it was necessary to make compromises between these two goals. In the virtual world, however, connections can be made easily between documents which might be physically distant from one another.

Historically, physical or bibliographic description preceded intellectual or subject description. Documents were originally listed in the same manner as gloves or chairs – an inventory of things. Bibliographic description includes the 'physical' details – author, title, date, publisher, edition, pagination, illustration and any other characteristic considered to be a useful identifier. Bibliographic description is well covered by the huge machinery of international codes and practices. The identification and recording of these elements with in relation to entirely web-based documents, such as transaction records and home pages, is under investigation through the Dublin Core suite of conferences and publications.

Intellectual or content representation

Organising structures such as classification schemes and thesauri are devised to provide access to the content of documents or the information itself. Indexing involves describing these concepts using either the language of the document itself, or by using a controlled language which will hopefully match up with the expression of a user's request. Classification involves using alphabetical, numeric or alphanumeric systems which represent information, and allow for the sequential linear arrangement of physical documents.

As Alfred Korzybski once stated, 'The map is not the territory, and the name is not the thing named' (Korzybski, 1994). Applying words, numbers or letters to represent information, there is another movement away from the actual ideas conceived by the creator of information. Gregory Bateson, in *Steps to an Ecology of Mind* (1973), elucidates the essential impossibility of knowing what the territory [information] is, as any understanding of it is based on some representation. Firstly, the creator has expressed ideas in some form – which might be written or spoken language, song, dance, signs, images, mathematics or pictures. Human experience is multisensory, and thought representation is subject to the constraints of the medium (language, music, mathematics and so forth). Sometimes we cannot use words (signs, gestures, dance, pictures need to suffice). It is next to impossible to convey smell, colour or touch except by comparison.

The ideas, having been translated into a medium of communication, have in turn to be understood and have meaning for the reader/viewer. The intermediary, as a reader/viewer, then summarises the concepts into a code, which, it is optimistically hoped, will be similar to a code which the information seeker might use to locate the creator's ideas.

In order to understand how ideas can be expressed, and how these expressions can in turn be described in order to identify and distinguish them (as well as possibly locating them), IPs have to understand the role of language and communication.

Language comprises two major aspects: words which have meanings (semantics) and the relationship between words (syntactics). Languages are generally public, in that, by using them, we are able to convey meaning through making sense. Language can be used to understand reality or to be deliberately obscure and confusing.

The social construction of knowledge can be understood in terms of the Sapir-Whorf hypothesis, which argues that our thinking is shaped by the language we speak (this would include both the semantic and syntactic aspects). Chandler indicates the two central principles: 'According to the first, linguistic determinism, our thinking is determined by language. According to the second, linguistic relativity, people who speak different languages perceive and think about the world quite differently' (Chandler, 1994).

Tenkasi and Boland add that 'We can only grasp reality through the various descriptions and classificatory mechanisms afforded by our language games. They provide us with the conceptual apparatus (rules, meanings, conventions) that constitutes our perceptual possibilities' (Tenkasi and Boland, 1998). This suggests an ineffable link between knowledge and language.

Words convey meaning, but will only do so if there exist mutual belief systems which are, in turn, culturally constructed. The relationship between words (whether written or spoken) is arbitrary: words are inherently symbolic, and yet language is constantly changing, both semantically and syntactically. This makes possible expressions of great complexity, abstraction and subtle nuance, and also confusion and error. Wittgenstein explored the meaning of words and sentences in order to determine whether there was logic and stability in their meaning, so that they could be used unambiguously to convey information. Wittgenstein determined that there was no difference between clocks and clouds.

> [H]e came to see how words and sentences did not have a characteristic internal structure and the meaning of words is specified by the rules of intelligibility embedded in the institutional context in which language is

employed. Further, he realized that these linguistic referents are the vehicles of our knowledge and comprehension of the world. We perceive nothing except through the meaning structures of our language in which perception and knowledge is embedded. (Tenkasi and Boland, 1998)

Frege considered that the meaning of a name is not the thing it refers to – meaning is the sense of the word (Carl, 1994). Two names for the same thing can have different senses, such as a first name and a nickname for a person, or slang. Sense is something possessed by a word, regardless of whether it has a reference. Sense and reference correspond to the connotation and denotation, or the intension and extension of an expression. The connotation of a word is the attribute or attributes implied by the name; the denotation of a word is any object to which the name applies.

Semantics focuses on what words mean, syntactics refers to the structural relations between words and signs, and pragmatics indicates the relation of signs to interpreters (or how context can change the meaning of words), while semiotics is concerned with how signs mean. These are all branches of linguistics. Linguistics is the science of language, which makes distinctions between the sign, the signifiers and the signifieds.

In the area of knowledge representation, it is necessary to know something of the following:

- communication studies – particular contextualised communication models;

- philosophy: the principle of universals, ontologies and taxonomies, philosophy of language;

- postmodernist understanding of perspectives and multiple simultaneous realities;

- the structure and analysis of words and how they convey meaning and make sense – syntactics, semantics, pragmatics and semiotics.

- social construction of knowledge and categorisation, mental models and frames of reference.

Human information behaviour

It is an absolutely primary requirement for the new IP to understand how and why humans seek and use information. This seldom formed a part of library school curricula until the past few years. It was preceded by an area known as 'User Studies' which, while closely aligned, examined the users of information systems in terms of broad demographic descriptors – it did not engage with reasons why information systems were used or avoided. The objective of user studies was to assess the informational, educational and recreational needs of diverse users and provide information services and resources appropriate to those needs. The results, however, tended to be generalised.

This view of information users led to a construction of a user as someone deficient, lacking, needy, uninformed, ignorant and so forth. It has more recently been recognised that what is required is a more profound understanding of the cognitive, affective and social processes underlying information needs, searching, interpreting and problem-solving, and how people attempt to understand reality. However, the basic premise is still that of a user having 'information needs' which are the initiator of any information search, which is likely not appropriate in either breadth or depth, or perhaps a different word ('motivation'?) is required.

It is also generally understood that information needs arise because of the more generalised need to solve problems. It is important to differentiate between those problems which individuals encounter for which information is useful in determining a solution, and those where it is not. This distinction is not always made.

Some problems require interventions by other kinds of professionals, who in turn will rely on information in order to assist in their solution. This occurs when the information available is too complex to be interpreted by somebody not familiar with the discourses and language of the information, and it requires the accumulated knowledge of a specialist in the area for interpretation and application. While the new IP's area of expertise is information, this does not mean that the new IP is expected to be, or can be, an expert in every field of knowledge.

Understanding human information behaviour (HIB) has paradoxically become more, rather than less, important with the easy accessibility of information through ICTs. Information overload is an increasing problem for users, due in part to their lack of skills; they generally lack the ability (or patience) to assess and evaluate retrieved information and are often unaware of this deficit. The problem of information overload is undertheorised, as it is a term used to indicate data or sensory overload as well. 'Information overload' most commonly refers to too much redundant, irrelevant, repetitive or superfluous information, but the question needs to be asked: for whom? There are subjective differences in the assessment of this occurrence.

Besides the deluge of information available through the ICTs, there is a plethora available through the media. Production of information grows far more rapidly than consumption, in spite of a seemingly insatiable appetite for information. There is a growing inability to focus on one issue. This resonates with Baudrillard's statement that 'We are in a universe where there is more and more information, and less and less meaning' (Baudrillard, 1983).

The quantity of information means little; it is the qualitative attributes that are valuable. There is more of an onus on the new IP to intervene in the role of counsellor and guide to information – although this can, of course, only be performed if the IP possesses these skills. IPs, as intermediaries, can indicate information that is faulty, misleading, exaggerated or incomplete. Other factors that affect the usefulness of information include length, language, timeframe, medium and author.

They can also assist by providing a variety of points of view on a particular topic, including those that are critical and conflicting, promoting creativity, innovation and balanced views, even though these may differ from prevailing metanarratives. A corollary of this activity is expressed in the truism, 'You don't know what you don't know'. For many, the world of information available is only just being discovered through ICTs: it is almost as if information was invented by the Internet.

There is a shift concerning the role of information services in education, in that the present focus is on individuals acquiring information skills (often confusingly named 'information literacy' in order to engage in lifelong learning), now seen as a social and professional necessity. Information literacy courses tend to concentrate on the acquisition of the types of skills that IPs themselves possess, and success in this is both superficial and largely unsuccessful, particularly when such skills are not integrated into the mainstream of educational programmes. What is also deficient in such approaches is the neglect of the sophisticated area of information evaluation which, as has been proposed, is largely absent in many IPs themselves, because of the traditional emphasis on documents.

There has been increasing work in the area of HIB. For example, Kuhlthau's (1993) study of high-school students looked at both the actions and the affective responses to the actions of information retrieval, located in a specific environment. The work has provided a broad, theoretical underpinning for the information experiences of the group. Dervin discovered that for most daily information needs, people did not use libraries. Most people do not get the help they need for everyday problems from the various communication devices designed to provide knowledge and information to communities. Another area of HIB is information coordinating behaviour, which Spink defines as 'a reiterative process whereby users assess their own information-searching skills, their knowledge of the system and the resources they discover, combined with what they learn along the way' (Spink, 2000).

HIB includes the area of making meaning of the information retrieved, and Dervin's work in sense-making is of particular interest here. Unsurprisingly, she emerged from communication studies, which lends itself to such interpretations. Information seeking is a form of human behaviour in which people gather information in order to 'make sense' of their world (Dervin and Nilan, 1986). This gives an interesting view of the construction of 'information need'. The 'sense-making' model describes 'information seeking and use' behaviour as that in which people actively attempt to bridge cognitive gaps in their knowledge. The gaps may be of many different types and differently defined.

The context of information behaviour is another focus of HIB. Users must be able to interpret the new information in terms of their own unique frames of reference. This framework includes the view that individuals have of themselves, how they understand their environment, their past experiences, and concepts and objects with which they are familiar. Marchionini refers to this as a 'Personal Information Infrastructure' (Marchionini, 1995). Added to this, there are personality characteristics such as intelligence, patience and creativity which also determine the sense-making abilities of the user.

Underlying sense-making is the phenomenon of 'symbolic interaction', a term coined by Blumer. This refers to the human desire to interpret rather than just observe or react; human reaction is based on the meaning formed from interpretation. He notes that

> ... human interaction is mediated by the use of symbols, by interpretation, or by ascertaining the meaning of one another's actions. This mediation is equivalent to inserting a process of interpretation between stimulus and response in the case of human behaviour. (Blumer, 1937: 180)

Factors that affect information seeking include Zipf's Law ('An individual's entire behaviour is subject to the minimizing of effort', Zipf, 1949) and bounded rationality, which determines the simplification of a problem because it would be too difficult to explore all the alternative solutions. Searching for information becomes far more difficult and complex a task if the nature and structure of information, and its retrieval tools, are poorly understood.

Outcomes of the use of information might include problem-solving, entertainment, cultural enrichment, persuading others, winning arguments, decision-making or learning. An important concept at the heart of sense-making is 'cognitive movement' (Nilan and Rosenbaum, 1991). People move from one understanding to another, which they describe as '... a fundamental human condition in which new meanings are sought or obtained' (Nilan and Rosenbaum, 1991). Newby associates this determination of meaning with learning:

Cognitive movement might alternatively be called 'learning' (but without implying active information seeking by the learner), 'attitude change' (but referring to all that is known, not just attitudes ...), or simply 'change in knowledge' (but without implying that the change is great or significant, or even noticed). (Newby, 1993: 9)

These outcomes are strongly related to the idea of information as power. A way of assessing the value of information is to distinguish between the results of informed actions and the results of uninformed actions or no action. We believe it is preferable to have an educated, informed population rather than an illiterate and ignorant one – whether in countries or in organisations. The accumulation of knowledge through education, and the ability to solve problems and make strategic decisions, are often combined with the accumulation of material wealth (and hopefully spiritual wealth as well).

Disciplines and topics which contribute to the understanding of this area include:

- communication studies;
- cultural studies;
- psychology;
- learning theories;
- philosophy (especially hermeneutics);
- linguistics, particularly semiotics.

Information capture and communication

It is expected that the new IP will understand the nature, genesis, organisation, maintenance, use, evaluation and preservation of documents, as well as being knowledgeable about their format, content and function. The new IP must be able to distinguish between types of documents, from manuscripts and scrolls, to serials, series and objects. The idiosyncrasies of each will determine the best ways in which they might be managed, with particular regard to the information contained within them. Added to this, knowledge of the different types of information systems which contain or control information is also necessary.

Another aspect of communication studies which is relevant here is media theory: an examination of the media through which communication is possible, usually including radio, TV, performances, photography, film, computers and so on. Media theory itself draws on other disciplines, including gender studies, semiotics, postmodernism and visual theories. Interpretation of media other than text has become an integral part of the work of the new IP, who now needs to have a critical understanding of media institutions, technologies and content, as well as their effects on individuals and societies.

Document warehouses, such as libraries, registries and archives, are in effect part of such media – although this is once again seldom recognised in this way. The processes of document selection tend to reinforce certain views, or provide a framework for understanding, in much the same way as the mass media do, although such collections of documents are in a more powerful position to provide a range of different views.

Topics and disciplines that are essential to this area include:

- multimedia technologies;
- communication studies, media theory and uses of media, transmission models;

- cultural studies;

- preservation and conservation techniques;

- history;

- history of libraries and their roles in society;

- political science;

- literature;

- art, particularly visual arts;

- postmodernism;

- gender studies.

Social informatics

Because of the relationships between information and society, technology and information, and society and technology, a field which attempts to combine all of these which is of great interest to the new IP, and this is social informatics (SI). It comprises a body of research that specifically examines the social aspects of computerisation, and includes both the roles of IT in social and organisational change and the social forces and practices that influence technologies. SI is a multidisciplinary field which draws from information systems, computer science, communications, sociology, political science and library and information science, and which explores the design, uses and consequences of IT.

SI acknowledges that IT is neither designed nor used in social or technological isolation (Kling, 1997). Kling notes that technology has to be relevant to the sites of social practice, and the design and implementation of IT must be relevant to the lives of people (Kling, 2001).

A related area is participatory design. While most professional literature still defines user involvement as assessing user requirements for a system at the beginning of the design process, and then observing how people in fact use the system, participatory design involves people through all stages. This has emerged partly from the realisation that people and groups use ICTs in a variety of creative ways, unanticipated by designers. It also recognises that the onus is on designers to match user requirements, rather than users learning how to use the system adequately.

The following areas are useful in understanding social informatics:

- information systems analysis and design;
- communication;
- semiotics;
- organisational communication;
- technological literacy.

Role of information in society and social responsibilities

Information plays a role in the creation or production of knowledge in all formal disciplines, and knowledges outside of these, such as of informal subcultures and indigenous peoples, are also within the ambit of the new IP. A slightly different slant is now taken: the role that information can play in shaping, forming and influencing individuals, organisations and society. The world of human activity includes the cultural, financial, academic, industrial, political commercial, institutional, educational, spiritual, philosophical and artistic, and information and its communication are central to all of these activities.

The discussion above concerning epistemologies and discourses was primarily concerned with the influence of society and social norms upon the creation and understanding of knowledge. Almost the reverse is social epistemology (SE), a phrase coined by Shera and defined by him as '... the study of knowledge in society ... The focus of this discipline should be upon the production, flow, integration, and consumption of all forms of communicated thought throughout the entire social fabric' (Shera, 1970: 86). It emphasises the use, rather than creation, of knowledge, even though it can be assumed that there is interaction between these two elements. It is important to note this distinction. The development of SE has gradually changed so that now its perspective appears to more closely resemble that of the sociology of knowledge and how knowledge develops in social contexts (e.g. Goldman, 1999), but this is quite different.

The narrow version of Shera's understanding of the term would concentrate on the uses made of information within society, and examine issues such as accessibility, media and perhaps information economics. A wider understanding, however, makes it clear that the new IP has social responsibilities regarding the use and communication of information.

Foucault has noted that the constitution of 'a specific field of knowledge is a political act which simultaneously configures a field of ignorance' (Foucault, 1984: 381). The apparent avoidance of values is a value commitment in itself. Libraries, archives and records registries have generally adopted and represented the opinions of the larger organisations of which they are a part. In the case of public libraries, the prevailing public ethos is represented, generally favouring an elite or, at best, a middle-class view. In their association with Putnam's view of social capital, they can be seen as modernist institutions.

Should the IP ideology support only wealth creation in northern, powerful nations? Probably not, for two reasons: this constructs any other social objective as 'other' and 'disprivileged'. Different cultures may be viewed as superficial or even irrelevant, and the penetration of western ideologies may not be possible or appropriate. Secondly, some of the effects of the powerful globalised communication media which possibly reinforce these views can be counteracted by IPs who adopt pluralist perspectives and expand communication strategies and information resources. Cultural and ideological differences may be better understood, and diversity better understood and enjoyed. As the Design for Social Change group has noted, 'What's more important to society's pillars is not what they hold up but what they stand on' (Design for Social Change, 2002). This suggests the importance of sustainability.

Some believe that the ultimate mark of a profession is having statutory recognition of practice, but a truly distinguishing characteristic is that it fulfils a social role and has social responsibilities which explain why the work is done at all. For the IPs, this role has expanded beyond mere access to information, although this will continue to be important, and must now include extended social responsibilities. Information management cannot be a neutral social science, as professional tasks take place within larger educational, political and cultural contexts, where any action, even no action, is political.

For example, the notion of 'information rich' and 'information poor', which has now been transformed into the phrase 'digital divide', is based on a supposition that those who have more information are also likely to be wealthier in economic terms. This nullifies the concept of indigenous and local knowledges, dismissing them as inferior or irrelevant. Not only might these knowledges be of some use (economic or otherwise) to prevailing elites; these knowledges have value to the communities in which they reside and are therefore valuable.

If information is perceived as a social good, the processes of commercialisation and privatisation which commodify information must be resisted – and IPs can play a role in this as information becomes more expensive, particularly to those who already lack basic telecommunications and electrical infrastructures.

Access to ICTs is not global or democratic, as noted. Theoretically ICTs can build a worldwide network that breaks down the boundaries between countries and removes the barriers between people from different cultures. In reality, this is not the case: while there are six billion people on the planet, not even one billion have regular access to the Internet, and are not likely to in their lifetimes. What might soon become an associated necessity is the ability of IPs to speak, read and write at least one other language.

As some wag noted, 'If information is power, why don't librarians rule the world?' It is quite clear they don't: IPs largely lack political acumen and are seldom politically active. The strongest link between economics and the world is politics. The political economy of information is interested in the ways that communicative activity is structured by the unequal distribution of material and symbolic resources. Power is exercised in and through the social relations mediated by information; dominance over information is achieved and maintained by specific groups, and specific forms of dominance such as race, class and gender are implicated in the exercise of power over information. Those who have the power are those that use the information.

Frohmann's view is that we have either ignored our political role, or we have tacitly agreed to prevailing exercises of power:

> A reflexive critique in IS would show how IS theories, through their contesting definitions and theoretical constructions of information, information user, information need and the like, enable specific institutional exercise of power over the production, organisation, distribution and consumption of information. (Frohmann, 1992)

Some indication has been given above of the potential political role IPs can play. This is reinforced in the archival world by An, who points out:

> Postmodern archival thinking considers archiving to be a key feature of society's communication processes in shaping the reality rather than just documenting it. It views archivists as co-creators of knowledge, culture and society rather than just passive recipients merely guarding and retrieving records and knowledge created entirely by others. (An, 2001)

The social role of IPs is related to a broader understanding of politics, economics and globalisation. Organisational informatics researchers have found that many ICTs actually can shift the balance of influence and power in organisations by restructuring access to information and through the kind of legitimacy that informational resources can bring (e.g. Danziger et al., 1982), and this is probably true in society as a whole.

Information policy development is related to this, be it at an organisational, governmental or even international level. Frohmann's work is once again interesting here: he has stated that 'The description of an information policy therefore becomes the description of the genealogy of a regime of information' (Frohmann, 1995). He continued, in 1996:

A legitimate and pressing objective of information policy research is the perspicuous representation of regimes of information: how they originate and stabilize, how they determine social relations, and how specific forms of power are exercised in and through them. The description of an information policy therefore becomes the description of the genealogy of a regime of information. Because it recognizes that information policy is made and unmade every day in complex, interacting social practices, research of this kind transcends LIS's narrow disciplinary conceptions of IP. (Frohmann, 1996)

Birdsall (1994) is in favour of increasing politicisation of IPs. He notes: 'There has been little sustained critical inquiry within librarianship of the premises upon which much government economic policy is founded' (Birdsall, 1994). There is a marked lack of either research or involvement in this area, whereas, in terms of social responsibilities, it is of central concern to information management. If IPs are to ensure access to a wide range of materials in order to support favourable outcomes from the use of information, a conceptual framework must be developed which will assist in the formulation of appropriate strategies.

Connected to the economic and political role of information are the associated areas of legislation and ethics. It is not possible in a work such as this to list all the laws that pertain to IPs, but it is necessary to observe that IPs are seldom involved in their formulation but must be concerned with their observance. It is also worth noting that each professional association in the information professions has developed its own set of professional ethics.

In addition, legislation is often enacted after information-based crimes have been perpetrated, because of rapid shifts and changes in ICTs. Information behaviour, for the public as well as IPs, needs to be guided by a communal understanding of what is ethically right – essentially knowing what is right and wrong. To act ethically, an ethical problem must be recognised. This is particularly relevant in the case of records managers, where records can be used as evidence in a court of law. However, there are many ethical issues, including copyright, intellectual property, privacy, surveillance, freedom of information and so forth.

Professional ethics specifically relates to the conduct of the IP professional in the course of duty, and these often go beyond the personal moral obligations of individuals, as is illustrated in medical circles by the euthanasia debate. In an increasingly complex and technologically dependent society, many critical issues relevant to information access and usage are misunderstood, overlooked or simply ignored, putting IPs in vulnerable positions.

Relevant disciplines and areas here include:

■ economics;

■ politics;

■ information technology;

■ law.

Where individual disciplines have been mentioned, a number of possibilities exist in order to incorporate them. Firstly, it is desirable that the information professions increasingly attract people from across the spectrum, and not rely so heavily on HSS graduates. In this way, a number of new IPs will have examined these areas as part of their undergraduate education. Secondly, research projects can be articulated across a variety of institutions and include experts from a number of different fields in order to tackle specific information problems. Such fluid working teams are increasingly common as problems become more complex, and the information professions should not be an exception. Finally, the relevant elements and theories from the disciplines mentioned here should be introduced in a first professional qualification (which ideally should take place at a postgraduate level) so that details of specialised practice can be extrapolated from them.

9

What does the new IP look like?

A window of opportunity exists for information professionals to reposition themselves as leaders in the IS and achieve wider recognition, authority and compensation. They obviously need a level of expertise in dealing with information that surpasses that of the general population (or encroaching groups) in order to make their mark. Gililand-Swetland remarks that 'A new kind of professional is needed ... who can function effectively in the dynamic interdisciplinary information environment' (Gililand-Swetland, 2000). This requires both a deeper understanding of issues that are unique to the information professions as well as wider understanding of the role of information in society.

The growth area for careers for the IPs appears to be for the most part outside traditional information organisations. Organisations need sophisticated professionals with professional communication skills and the analytical ability to address complex managerial issues to assume leadership positions in information work. Alongside this, there will certainly continue to be jobs similar to the TIPs (even in a modified form), not only because paper and books will undoubtedly be around for a long time yet, but also because this work, as a sub-area of the new IP, will continue to have value to society and organisations.

Aims of the new IP

The aims of the new IP are, in general terms, broader than those of the specialisations that occur within the field. Mostly, these objectives are society-wide, although some of them may refer to organisations specifically:

- to increase the creativity and intelligence of workers and citizens so that they become problem-solvers, decision-makers and thinkers;

- to improve physical and intellectual access to information and documents;

- to develop and evaluate information resources and their use within organisations and throughout society at large;

- to encourage and support the strategic use of information in businesses, government and non-profit organisations for the development of social improvement and an informed population;

- to create information policies (for organisations and nations) that support equitable access to information and its associated technologies, so that the use of these resources can be maximised;

- to understand how and why information is searched for and used, so that assistance can be offered in these activities.

Competencies of the new IP

The new IP is called upon to address a number of information-related problems and thus the function is a complex one. Such issues include the social, cultural, economic, legal, strategic, educational, technological and organisational. The competencies of the new IP, relating to the professional approach and attitude, are stated here in general terms.

■ *Knowledge of how knowledge is created and produced.* New IPs are able to critically analyse information sources and resources, examining the motives behind the creation of knowledge and information, including locating this within political and social discourses. Indigenous and informal knowledge bases are included. This necessitates an understanding of social, literary and cultural issues, as well as of research methodologies.

■ *Emphasise information, rather than documents.* The concept of information resources is wide and all-embracing, and includes, *inter alia*, documents, dances, works of art, oral traditions, symbols and people as well as their supporting technologies. There is a proactive, rather than passive, approach to information provision. New IPs can sift and sort through documents, not only to locate pieces of information, but to put those pieces into context, and to weigh and compare different items, identify, authenticate and validate them, and interpret them to users.

■ *Appreciate the variety of information resources and know how to use them.* The new IP is able to under-stand the different values that individuals and social groups might place on different types or presentations of information, and ensures that compatibility is achieved in this regard.

■ *Human information behaviour.* A new IP has an understanding of how and why people search for infor-mation, how they evaluate that information when they stop looking, and how they use the information that they have found. New IPs are inclusive, concentrating on both actual and potential users. They can determine and understand information needs, use and applications, often by conducting analyses of information behaviour. New IPs are able to focus on the detail of specific situations, as well as locating them within a broader context.

- *Research*. New IPs are adept at both qualitative and quantitative research.

- *ICTs*. New IPs possess technological literacy and are able to adopt a critical and evaluative approach to ICTs and their use. New IPs know how information systems, in their broadest sense, work and are adept at their use. They are able to contribute to the development of information gateways and corporate portals, to design large-scale websites using information architecture and mapping skills, and to structure content and navigation flow.

- *Legal*. New IPs understand and fulfil the legal and statutory obligations which arise from holding and disseminating information, including the duty of care to third parties, intellectual property, intellectual capital, privacy, security, copyright and records compliance legislation.

In organisations, new IPs possess all the above competencies, and are able to perform the following work:

- identify, specify and map business and social processes and procedures and the manner in which information is used and manipulated within those processes;

- disseminate information within organisations and society at large but avoid information overload;

- support personal, governmental and managerial decisions with quality information;

- ensure that procedures and systems are in place for monitoring and auditing the quality of information management within government and business;

- provide cost savings in the procurement and handling of information;

- identify gaps in and duplication of information;

- clarify the roles and responsibilities of owners and users of information and identify information sources which might be relevant to the strategic direction of the individual, government or organisation;

- ensure the evaluation, development and implementation of best practice throughout organisations of all kinds;

- realise the value of presentation and visualisation of information;

- coordinate expenditure on information and assess information values[1] on personal, organisational, governmental and national levels, with particular regard to equity.

Personal competencies

There are particular skills, attitudes and values that new IPs have which contribute to and enhance their professional competencies. They are able to:

- solve problems;

- work in teams;

- embrace continuous change;

- engage in lifelong learning;

- have interdisciplinary knowledge, which may include knowledge of business, languages and other relevant knowledges;

- demonstrate commitment to service;
- have effective communication and interpersonal skills;
- be flexible;
- demonstrate high ethical standards in professional and personal life;
- possess an intellectual openness and curiosity and an appreciation of the interconnectedness and areas of uncertainty in current human knowledge;
- engage in critical, conceptual and reflective thinking in all aspects of intellectual and practical activity.

Careers for the new IP

It should be reiterated at this point that the areas of knowledge and topics that constitute the core knowledge for the new IP and the profile and abilities of the new IP have, up to this point, been generalised as a new metalevel of information practice in accordance with Meta-System Transition. Underneath this level, necessity demands that there will continue to be specialisations, some traditional and some new, and altogether a wider range than perhaps previously acknowledged in the contesting and separate independent development which has occurred thus far.

The foundation outlined above provides a base upon which to build the wide range of information professions at different levels which are demanded by society's complexity. However, specialisation should be encouraged at an advanced and not introductory level. More superficialists are not required, who have a smattering of bits and pieces of professional knowledge across a discipline that is too wide to capture within one year, even if this is at postgraduate level. Some possible specialisations are listed below.

Organisational information and document management

The information within organisations is generally differentiated into data (including financial, personnel, customer and supplier data), information (including both published and unpublished, and from internal as well as external resources), documents and knowledge (what the employees know about the work and processes of the organisation).

Data management

Data management is responsible for a wide range of functions, including database planning, analysis, design, implementation, maintenance and protection. Also, data management involves the tasks of improving database performance and providing education, training and consulting support to users. It is usual for the IT function to perform the associated tasks, although IPs are involved in at least two aspects, namely metadata management and exploring the possibilities of data mining.

Document management

An extraordinary number of documents are produced during the course of daily business within an organisation, of which many are still on paper. Managing these documents (and of course the information they contain) is vital, as the inability to find documents can be very expensive, either because workflow is disrupted or because an organisation consequently becomes liable for litigation. Controlling the number of copies of documents is another element of this area, as physical storage in particular is very expensive and can also allow misuse of information.

Records management

Among all these documents, records must be identified. Records provide evidence of the business transactions of the organisation, as well as facilitating its work. They must be integrated and compatible with the broader ethos of information accumulation, handling, storing and organisation that occurs, so that other functions of the organisation can succeed. Records, as documents which contain information, also have uses in terms of achieving the goals of the organisation. However, records management has a broader social obligation in terms of supporting anti-corruption legislation and ensuring accountability of organisations and governments to their constituencies, including employees.

Archives

Associated with records management are archives, although today the distinctions between the two areas are steadily blurring. Essentially, archives contain those records which are no longer in current use, but are perceived to have a wider historical or social value and therefore need to be preserved for anticipated future use. Determining which records must be kept is a complicated task, as is the preservation of old and fragile materials and the new problems of preserving digital materials in an ever-changing virtual environment. Archives assist in the preservation of corporate and social memory: their political and social obligation is to preserve all points of view at an historical moment and not just the 'party line'.

Corporate memory

Corporate memory is understood to include the documents, records and archives produced by an organisation as well as the knowledge contained within employees' heads. It does not include all information resources, and excludes published materials and ICTs, except to the extent that they capture or store corporate memory. The preservation and maintenance of corporate memory occurs in two ways: through the processes of archive administration as well as through the learning organisation (which contributes to KM).

Strategic information management

A strategy refers to a long-term plan for success and is frequently used in military and political circles. 'Strategic information' is information that can be used to develop or further a plan for success. An 'information strategy' is a plan for dealing with information successfully. 'Strategic information management' therefore involves using information in order to achieve these ends, and relates strongly to the possible uses that can be made of information, beyond merely storing it and making it accessible, by identifying, coordinating and coalescing information resources. Strategic information management is necessary at personal, organisational and government levels.

Knowledge management

Knowledge management is a complex, multidisciplinary area, as perhaps indicated by its seemingly oxymoronic name. It includes human resources (in order to build up communities and encourage knowledge sharing), management (to facilitate and reward constant learning and sharing of information), IT (to store, facilitate and map knowledge and information resources), strategic information management (to identify and use what is useful), human information behaviour (to understand how and why knowledge management process may be used), record-keeping, corporate memory (as base resources), organisational communication and business analysis.

Knowledge management, however, is very similar to information management in many respects, and has probably developed because of the overuse and misuse of the terms 'data' and 'information'. It has little to do with the creation or representation of knowledge in either the philosophical or linguistic senses, and is specifically related to business or organisational information rather than all types of information. Even though it may be embodied in a 'learning organisation', the literature of knowledge management ignores learning theories as a rule. As a field, it draws heavily on established and developing theory in the IPs.

The field of knowledge management can be approached from a cynical angle in that it views people as information containers (or documents) and seeks to exploit this resource for competitive advantage. This includes both employees and experts outside the organisation.

Competitive intelligence

Competitive intelligence (CI) refers to the process whereby public or published data is analysed to provide information and creates intelligence that is useful for decision-making. Intelligence describes information that has a direct use and application in the strategic management of an organisation. CI is distinguished by its interpretation of a wide variety of data and information resources, including advertisements, patents, company news, market reports and the like, and the creative activity involved in making meaning of these.

CI is also concerned with improving competitiveness, and thus an awareness of the competitive environment (including the political and demographic) and identification of major competitors and knowledge of their activities as well as industrial and market trends is essential. An essential tool in CI is environmental scanning, which is the process of monitoring changes and the rate of those changes in the external environment. While the term is similar to military intelligence, it does not involve spying, industrial espionage or any other illegal activity – it pays attention only to that information which is accessible to all.

The unique character of the activity lies in determining how, using various analytical techniques, all the information indicates a beneficial course of activity and is more than the random collection of facts or information. A corollary of CI is counter competitive intelligence – the mechanisms by which an organisation does not inadvertently reveal more than is intended and provide competitors with information that can be used against it.

Information audit

Conducting an information audit involves surveying all the information and knowledge resources of an organisation, as well as the information flows within it. An audit will reveal a relationship between the organisational structure and the information resources and how they are used. It also attempts to assess the attitudes and practices of employees and management with regard to information sources, and gathering and distributing information throughout the organisation. Systems analysis is a useful technique in the information audit.

The audit can be subdivided to cover the various areas of information within an organisation, including document, record, library or data audits, as well as information technologies. It seeks to identify bottlenecks and floods, gaps and duplications in both resources and flows. The audit frequently provides the basis for a reconsideration of information management activities and how better to use information, and frequently results in the development of an information policy. Its major value is that it serves to unify the concept of information throughout the organisation, government body or even state, and its value and cost may be appreciated. The results of an audit include an inventory as well as a description of the ecology of information flows and use.

Information policy

Being able to develop an information policy, for an organisation or a nation, is fast becoming an essential competency for new IPs. Information policy has been defined as 'the set of public laws, regulations and policies that encourage, discourage or regulate the creation, use, storage and communication of information'. Information policies therefore touch on a surprisingly wide range of aspects of life in modern society and their analysis can easily be seen to have political, social, economic and legal implications.

A policy is a useful standardising tool which creates routine ways of handling and treating information and has great value both for training staff and for fulfilling information requirements within organisations. Developing an information policy provides the opportunity to review current information practices, particularly in the light of achieving particular objectives, be these organisational or societal.

An information policy enables the maintenance of consistency of access, storage and retrieval conditions that are conducive to meeting information contingencies. It also provides the basis for objective decision-making on resources for information activities, particularly if it is integrated with a framework of objectives and priorities. On a national level, an information policy can be used for strategic development in many areas.

Information architecture

Information architecture (IA) is a discipline that involves designing the organisation, navigation, labelling and search mechanisms of information systems, where human factors are understood to be the determinants of success or failure. Rosenfeld and Morville define IA as '... the design or organization, labeling, navigation, and searching systems to help people find and manage information more successfully' (Rosenfeld and Morville, 2002: 23).

IA draws on established IP theory and practice (particularly the organisation of knowledge and information retrieval) to organise and represent information in hypertext networks. It is, once again and not surprisingly, a multidisciplinary area which includes principles from anthropology, human–computer interaction, graphic design, information retrieval, language and linguistics, metadata and semiotics.

It is different from the same phrase used by computer scientists to indicate the structure of databases. The word 'architecture' implies the concepts of structure and space, pleasing aesthetics and usefulness. It takes into account people, content and technology. In IA, there is a need to understand familiar IP functions such as the organisation of information and information representation, and also to have an understanding of how people search for information.

Libraries

There is, of course, a wide range of libraries, which, on the whole, are well discussed in the literature. These include corporate, public, national, medical, legal, state, academic, engineering, art, school, museum, parliamentary, music, newspaper, toy and digital libraries. Each of these libraries, like the specialisations named above, has associated special skills. For example, work in a manuscript collection will require advanced skills in systematic bibliography, while in an art library, some knowledge of artists, formats, historical periods, galleries and the like is required in order to deal with the varied range of materials. Space does not permit an in-depth discussion of these: suffice it to say that all of these skills are based on aspects of the core knowledge suggested above.

However, it must be remembered that many libraries now incorporate and make use of many digital resources, including catalogues, e-publications and digital downloads. This puts them in the same band of accessibility as any other networked information resource, against whom they are, in fact, competing. This opens up a range of new roles within libraries, most of which are still to be developed. For example, few libraries suggest additional materials to you, based on your searches and selections, in the same way as *Amazon.com*; sophisticated searching of library holdings is only available through e-serial aggregators such as Ebsco, although there are many endeavours, such as Project Gutenberg and the new Google venture, which are engaged in digitising the world's literature.

Libraries generally also make use of commercial services to provide alerts to recently published or acquired materials, along the lines of the old idea of selective dissemination of information (SDI). Designing and incorporating such services into existing academic, corporate, special and even school libraries, which have fairly well-defined clienteles, would be useful to promote both the library and the profession.

It is ironic that as information systems increase in number and complexity, library users are increasingly left to fend for themselves. The current focus on information literacy as a mechanism to use these systems skilfully cannot, I believe, succeed in the long run, as it is difficult enough for trained professionals to keep abreast of developments. Users should not be forced into this (rather unsatisfactory) self-service mode: they might as well stay at home and use Google, however ineptly. This reticence by librarians will probably make them even more invisible, and their mission more recondite.

From these comments, a further number of possible career paths can be identified. Among others, experienced and highly competent network navigators who are able to use a variety of search engines and reference sources available on the Web, including the Invisible Web and subject-specific resources, would be useful either attached to libraries or working as independent consultants and researchers attached to a variety of organisations. Digital outreach programmes which decentralise government, health and education information and assist in constructing information communities are also required, particularly in the majority world.

Information interventionists, who facilitate more informal information flows within communities of all kinds (urban, rural and organisational), would also find a great deal of work by establishing what information is required, and when, and to prevent the dissemination of misinformation, disinformation and inaccurate information. The library is no longer a place or space; digitised documents do not need a warehouse; community information kiosks which provide immediately useful information may well prove more beneficial than the provision of entertainment.

Another type of work which could be performed by information interventionists includes assisting users in making sense and meaning of information, whatever this might require, as well as indicating the point at which other professionals (doctors, lawyers, social workers and the like) are required – and provide information on how to contact them.

While over the past fifteen years or so much has been written about the possible career of information broker, there have been very few success stories, making it an unpredictable career choice as long as the full value of information itself is not widely recognised. It would appear that this kind of work is better performed as a particular role within government or an organisation, either managing the information necessary for the organisation itself or being engaged in the service delivery or product development work of the enterprise.

These are all sophisticated tasks which cannot be performed without specialist skills – but all require a heightened awareness of the potential value of information and its power.

Note

1. Gorman and Corbitt (2002) also provide a useful, but somewhat lengthier, list of competencies to be developed in information management education.

10

Conclusions

The IPs have been presented with a challenge to which they have thus far only responded reactively, becoming followers rather than leaders in the IS. Even though the IS has been initiated by, and predicated upon, ICTs, it is information rather than technology alone which has the capacity to change society. While the definition of information itself will continue to be discussed, as is evidenced by the recent special issue of *Library Trends* (2004), the IPs can nonetheless play a more prominent role without a final definition of this term, as long as a practicable contextualised mutually comprehensible understanding is agreed upon.

Information may be located on a plan of knowledge as either a roof or a floor: it is a thematic discipline in that it is aconstant in all knowledges. The very concepts of data, information and knowledge suggest an integrated, interdisciplinary approach to the IPs. Interdisciplinarity, perhaps more difficult than multidisciplinarity, is suggested in order to draw on theories that have already been explored in other areas. Interdisciplinarity cannot, however, be achieved within the scientific paradigm, and thus postmodernism and qualitative research methodologies are suggested. Synthesis rather than analysis will be more useful.

The purpose of knowledge is understanding; the purpose of information is comprehension. It is ironic, therefore, that in a quest for understanding and comprehension there is a reliance on technology rather than information itself.

Technology itself is neither threat nor promise. All knowledge can only be related in a multidisciplinary fashion through information; all knowledge and information have their basis in philosophy. As Floriadi has suggested, the IPs should develop their professional foundation in terms of a philosophy of information (Floriadi, 2004); another approach would be to embrace social epistemology more completely. Perhaps a combination of the two is appropriate. Whichever route unfolds, a foundation of enquiry should exist in order to explain and validate professional practices.

Perhaps now is the time for all good IPs to come to the aid of the metaphysical system-philosophers and enunciate the universality of information (and its communication and management). This is, as indicated, beyond the scope of this work, and discussion will undoubtedly continue for some time to come. However, as the concept of a metatheory has been discussed, it is useful to consider the philosophical approach:

> Metaphysical system-philosophers have always sought for ultimate unities, for ultimate principles to unify all knowledge. They sought for the fewest, simplest, and clearest keyword-principles to relate, explain, and unify the most knowledge; and which would resolve the most conflicts of truth, morality, justice and beauty. They sought such principles by logical induction; from facts to concepts, to principles; and by deduction from principles to concepts to facts. Some of these philosophers and their ultimate principles are: Socrates' Universals, Plato's Ideas, Aristotle's Categories, Plotinus's One, Kant's Categories, Hegel's Absolute, and Spencer's First Principles. (Bartek, 1998)

IPs need to engage more fully with the complexity of human activities: they cannot find the answers they seek within the present structure of the TIPs; however, the integrity of the professions lends itself to this activity. This should result in a more complete user-centred approach. In addition to this, attention must be paid to new generations which have different literacies and different understandings of the role of information in their lives (e.g. Tapscott, 1999). This should include understanding of majority world populations as well.

While libraries of all types will undoubtedly continue to exist and require professionals to staff them, information work in general can be uncoupled from such institutions and in so doing may be better understood as supporting a wider range of human activities. An abstraction of the knowledge base to include a wider and holistic view of information work in all sorts of places and under all sorts of conditions would better prepare IPs for the complex world in which we live. Much work that is now required is nothing like the work done in libraries; the metasystemic core knowledge suggested here will prepare IPs to take advantage of the many more opportunities that are now available.

I have likened IPs to artists and considered their role as philosophers. Underlying this is a tacit endorsement of Buckland's view (1996) of information work as a liberal art, where the subject itself is studied, rather than the specific skills that are required to execute professional tasks. He asks revealingly: 'What about LIS for people who have no intention of LIS employment?' (Buckland, 1996). By the same token, it can be argued that the subject matter of the IPs should be integrated into all education, across all disciplines. A corollary to this is further examination of the role of information in society and how its outcomes can be identified.

The model of practice can likewise change. Instead of the IP being in the position of serving the disparate information needs of large heterogenous communities, perhaps the model used in other professions, such as medicine, architecture or law, can be copied, where there is a one-on-one client/professional relationship, and each client receives individual and customised attention. This will permit a clearer distinction between professional and para-professional work, while simultaneously acknowledging the essential, but different, role of library technicians.

The education of skilled information professionals is fortunately evolving to meet the many new challenges that have resulted from the complex, knowledge-based environment in which we live and work. At the same time, these programmes should engage students in responsible social and cultural analysis and debate.

As Francis Picabia, a French Dadaist who lived from 1869 to 1953, once noted, 'Heads are round so our thinking can change direction'.

Appendix

What do organisations want from IPs?

The advertisements considered here appeared in *The Australian* (a national newspaper in Australia), *The Advertiser* (a South Australian newspaper) and announcements posted on ASIS-L, PACS-L, RECMGMT-L and RMAA-list, which are information-related listservs on the Internet. Specifically, the competencies demanded for each job were analysed and considered rather than job titles (which were viewed as often misleading and uninformative).

During this period, hundreds of such advertisements were collected, but a random sample of only 76 advertisements was taken for the purpose of this analysis. From them, phrases and terminology were drawn which described the characteristics and qualifications of the kind of staff they were looking for. Apart from an attempt to group these broadly under the subheadings given in Table A.1 no other attempt was made to rephrase the specifications. Phrases and terminology were drawn which described the characteristics and qualifications of the kind of staff they were looking for. One problem with this of course is that the terms are not exclusive, and there are some overlaps in meaning. One may presume that there are equally differences in the exact competencies required. The qualities as specified in the advertisements were then 'dropped' into these self-generative categories. While only 76 advertisements form the basis for this study, a scan of those omitted seemed to reveal great repetition and consistency with the figures reported here.

Table A.1	Analysis of characteristics of advertisements for information professionals

Attribute	Frequency
N = 76	
Management expertise	
Management of organisation; managing budgets and staff	11
Develop and implement procedural and policy initiatives and corporate strategies	10
Lead and manage staff	16
Build and implement a vision for the future sustainability of the service; vision and leadership in formulating programmes and implementing strategies	12
Project management	6
Technological expertise	
Assessment, implementation and monitoring of new technological systems	12
Technological expertise and understanding	11
Development and maintenance of Internet site	12
Knowledge of software and relational databases; ability to create data structures which facilitate the indexing and retrieval of information	15
Communication skills base	
High-level communication and interpersonal skills; strong conceptual, organisational, financial analysis, and oral and written skills, sound analytical and writing skills	37
Analysis and problem-solving skills; ability to perceive and analyse problems, develop alternatives and make recommendations; analytical skills	14
Capacity to undertake research and reviews, prepare reports	13
Give presentations on library services	6
Theoretical base required	
Assessment of the needs and usage styles of consumers of digital media	18
Textual contextual analysis	6
Knowledge of contemporary learning theories	2
Interpersonal communication and the creative process	4
Social impact of information and communication technologies	11
Effect of ICT on the development and conduct of scientific research	10

Table A.1 (continued)	
Attribute	**Frequency**
Role of information in national/international development	4
Personality features	
Working under pressure	7
Teamwork orientation	10
Self-motivation and the ability to work independently	6
Work through the direction of others	1
Passion for details	3
Professional information management skills	
Interpret and apply legislation and regulation	14
Knowledge of records management principles and electronic record-keeping	13
Reference and classroom instruction	9
Knowledge of electronic/multimedia resources	12
General records/information and business procedures; understand the interplay between the information and business needs of large companies	10
Experts in development of online search strategies	3
Digital resource management	5
Knowledge of AACR2, MARC formats and metadata standards	3

It is important to note that these results must be viewed relatively rather than absolutely, as of course across such a grouping much granularity and differentiation is lost.

These figures do not give an absolute or statistically meaningful analysis, but serve only to show the ordinal relations between the elements and the emphasis on qualities, skills and competencies detailed in the advertisements.

There is clear emphasis on elements which are not the basic skills or competencies which are usually taught in professional programmes for the information professions, and this is correlated by the low priority given to the professional body of knowledge. Another interesting emphasis is on knowledge of the legal implications of information work. Aspects considered important include developing strategies for developing future visions, analytical and problem-solving skills and understanding research processes.

Very few of the advertisements required their information professional to have managerial skills. It can only be assumed that most of these positions were line functions rather than leadership or specialist areas. Having said that, there were a number that required creative input regarding the future operation of the information service. It is interesting to note that skills were required to install new systems, build websites and construct and use databases. All of these are rather general technological skills.

Over half the advertisements demanded outstanding communication skills, including talking, reading and writing. Associated with these are analytical and problem-solving skills as well as the ability to do research. The emphasis on these is no surprise as information professionals are required not only to work with each other but with their managers and their users.

The nature and scope of the theoretical base desired is particularly fascinating. The understanding of human information behaviour is high on the list in the form of identifying what information people ('consumers') want and how they go about getting it, particularly using ICTs. A much broader view is required of the ways and means in which information is identified, organised and disseminated, as well as an emphasis on understanding the nature and flows of information, its societal influences, how it is created and the relationship between information and technology.

Added to this, knowledge of the content of documents is also required. The knowledge of contemporary learning theories was unexpected, although, on reflection, it appears quite appropriate. The function and nature of knowledge creation, information as a commodity in economics and the effects of ICT are also highlighted. It would appear that there is a demand by employers for information professionals whose knowledge of information problems is broader than usually conceived; in addition, there appears to be an understanding by these employers that a broad, yet unified, theoretical base would be useful to them, rather than a diffuse, fragmented, although specialised, one.

What is remarkable about these results is the generally infrequent or low rating of various aspects of what are generally considered to be 'core' professional skills and competencies. Among these, there is clear emphasis on the management of corporate information, as shown in the demand for records management expertise and knowledge of business.

References

Abbott, Andrew (1998) 'Professionalism and the future of librarianship', *Library Trends*, 46 (3): 430–44.

Agre, Philip (1995) 'Institutional circuitry: thinking about the forms and uses of information', *Information Technology and Libraries*, 14 (4): 225–30 (online at *http://polaris.gseis.ucla.edu/pagre/circuitry.html*).

Alderman, B. (2002) 'Marketing our image', *Access*, November: 12–15.

Allen, Bryce (1996) *Information Tasks: Toward a User-Centered Approach to Information Systems*. New York: Academic Press.

Alliance of Libraries, Archives and Records Management (2000) 'Competency profile: information resources management specialists in archives, libraries and records management: a comprehensive cross-sectoral competency analysis' (online at *http://www.cla.ca/resources/competency.htm*).

An, Xiomi (2001) 'A Chinese view of records continuum methodology and implications for managing electronic records' (online at *http://www.caldeson.com/RIMOS/Xanuum.html*).

Anderson, Elizabeth (2001) 'Feminist epistemology', *Stanford Encyclopedia of Philosophy* (online at *http://plato.stanford.edu/entries/feminism-epistemology/*).

Appignanesi, Richard and Garratt, Chris (1995) *Postmodernism for Beginners*. Cambridge: Icon.

Association for Library and Information Science Education (ALISE) (2000) *Educating Library and Information Science Professionals for a New Century: The KALIPER Report: Executive Summary*, July. Reston, VA: ALISE.

Australian Council of Professions (2003) *Constitution* (online at *http://www.professions.com.au/Constitution.html*).

Bains, Simon (1997) 'End-user searching behavior: considering methodologies' (online at *http://www.lis.uiuc.edu/review/winter1997/bains.html*).

Baldwin, J.M. (1957) *Dictionary of Philosophy and Psychology*. Gloucester: Macmillan.

Balsamo, Anne (1996) *Technologies of the Gendered Body: Reading Cyborg Women*. Durham, NC: Duke University Press.

Bangemann, M. (1994) *Europe and the Global Information Society: Recommendations to the European Council, Brussels*. Brussels: EC.

Barlow, John Perry (1994) *Themes for the 21st Century: Where Are We Going?* Speech presented at the mid-year meeting of the American Society for Information Science, Portland, OR, May 1994 (quoted by Van House, 1996).

Barnes, B. and Bloor, D. (1982) 'Relativism, rationalism and the sociology of knowledge', in M. Hollis and S. Lukes (eds), *Rationality and Relativism*. Oxford: Blackwell, pp. 21–47.

Bartek, Edward J. (1998) 'A global theory of knowledge for the future', in Twentieth World Congress of Philosophy, Boston, Massachusetts, 10–15 August (online at *http://www.bu.edu/wcp/Papers/TKno/TKnoBart.htm*).

Barthes, Roland (1972) *Mythologies*. New York: Hill & Wang.

Bateson, Gregory (1973) *Steps to an Ecology of Mind*. New York: Paladin Books.

Bateson, Gregory (1980) *Mind and Nature: A Necessary Unity*. New York: Bantam Books.

Baudrillard, Jean (1983) *In the Shadow of the Silent Majorities*. Cambridge, MA: Semiotext(e)/MIT Press.

Baudrillard, Jean (1994) *Simulacra and Simulation*, trans. Sheila Favia Glaser. Ann Arbor, MI: University of Michigan Press.

Beaumont, John R. and Sutherland, Ewan (1992) *Information Resources Management: Management in Our Knowledge-Based Society and Economy*. Oxford: Butterworth-Heinemann.

Becher, T. (1989) *Academic Tribes and Territories*. Buckingham: Open University Press.

Belkin, N.J. (1980) 'Anomalous States of Knowledge as a basis for information retrieval', *Canadian Journal of Information Science*, 5: 133–43.

Bell, Daniel (1974) *The Coming of the Post-industrial Society: A Venture in Social Forecasting*. London: Heinemann.

Bent, Dale H. (1995) 'Changing attitudes toward information management: they just don't seem to get it' (online at *http://www.cais-acsi.ca/proceedings/1995/bent_1995.pdf*).

Berger, Peter L. and Luckmann, Thomas (1966) *The Social Construction of Reality*. New York: Doubleday.

Best, David P. (ed.) (1996) *The Fourth Resource: Information and Its Management*. Aldershot: Gower.

Biglan, A. (1973) 'Relationships between subject matter characteristics and the structure and output of university departments', *Journal of Applied Psychology*, 57: 195–203.

Bijker, W.E. (1995) *Of Bicycles, Bakelites, and Bulbs: Toward a Theory of Sociotechnical Change*. Cambridge, MA: MIT Press.

Bijker, Wiebe and Law, John (1992) *Shaping Technology/Building Society: Studies in Sociotechnical Change*. Cambridge, MA: MIT Press.

Bijker, Wiebe, Hughes, Thomas P. and Pinch, Trevor (1989) *The Social Construction of Technological Systems*. Cambridge, MA: MIT Press.

Birdsall, William (1994) *The Myth of the Electronic Library: Librarianship and Social Change in America*. Connecticut: Greenwood Press.

Blackler, Frank (1995) 'Knowledge, knowledge work and organizations: an overview and interpretation', *Organization Studies*, 16 (6): 1021–47.

Bloor, D. (1991) *Knowledge and Social Imagery*, 2nd edn. Boston, MA: Routledge.

Blumer, Herbert (1937, 1969) *Symbolic Interactionism: Perspective and Method*. Englewood Cliffs, NJ: Prentice Hall (reissued by University of California Press).

Bourdieu, Pierre (1984) *Homo academicus*, trans. Peter Colliens. Stanford, CA: Stanford University Press.

Bourdieu, Pierre (1986) 'The forms of capital', in J.G. Richardson (ed.), *Handbook of Theory and Research for the Sociology of Education*. New York: Greenwood Press, pp. 241–58.

Bourdieu, Pierre (1990) *In Other Words: Essays Towards a Reflexive Sociology*, trans. Matthew Adamson. Stanford, CA: Stanford University Press.

Bourdieu, Pierre (1993) *The Field of Cultural Production*, ed. and intro. Randal Johnson. New York: Columbia University Press.

Bourdieu, Pierre and Wacquant, Loic J.D. (1992) *An Invitation to Reflexive Sociology*. Chicago: University of Chicago Press.

Bousquet, Marc and Wills, Katherine (eds) (2004) *The Politics of Information*. Alt-X (online at *http://www.altx.com/ebooks/ infopol.html*).

Braidotti, Rosi (1994) 'Ma come sono toste queste donne!: cyberfeminism with a difference' (online at *http://www .mediares.it/yanez/costume/pagina.htm*).

Braybrooke, D. and Lindblom, C.E. (1963) *A Strategy of Decision*. New York: Free Press.

Briet, Suzanne (1951) *Qu'est-ce que la documentation?* Paris: EDIT (online at *http://www.lisp.wayne.edu/~ai2398/briet.htm*).

Brittain, Michael (1995) 'New Job Opportunities for Information Professionals in Australia'. Adelaide: University of South Australia (unpublished).

Brockman, John (1996) *Digerati: Encounters with the Cyber Elite*. San Francisco: HardWired.

Brown-Syed, C. (1998) 'SOS calls, breaking stories, network disinformation, and the process of scholarly communication: implications for information intermediaries', *CAIS/ACSI '98: Information Science at the Dawn of the Next Millenium*. Toronto: Canadian Association for Information Science, pp. 429–45.

Buckland, Michael (1996) 'Documentation, information science, and library science in the U.S.A.', *Information Processing and Management*, 32 (1): 63–76.

Buckland, Michael Keeble (1988) *Library Services in Theory and Context*, 2nd edn. New York: Pergamon Press.

Budd, John M. (1999) 'The information professions as knowledge professions' (online at *http://conference99.fh-hannover.de/ fulltext/budd_f.htm*).

Budd, John M. and Raber, Douglas (1996) 'Discourse analysis: method and application in the study of information', *Information Processing and Management*, 32 (2): 217–26.

Burr, Vivien (1995) *An Introduction to Social Constructionism*. London: Routledge.

Butler, Pierce (1933) *An Introduction to Library Science*. Chicago: University of Chicago Press.

Capra, Fritjof (1975) *The Tao of Physics: An Exploration of the Parallels between Modern Physics and Eastern Mysticism*. London: Fontana.

Capra, Fritjof (1996) *The Web of Life: A New Scientific Understanding of Living Systems*. New York: Simon & Schuster.

Capurro, Rafael (1991) 'Foundations of information science: reviews and perspectives' (online *http://v.hbi-stuttgart.de/apurro/tampere91.htm*).

Capurro, Rafael (1996) 'On the genealogy of information', in K. Kornwachs and K. Jacoby (eds), *Information: New Questions to a Multidisciplinary Concept*. Berlin: Akademie Verlag.

Capurro, Rafael (2000) 'Hermeneutics and the phenomenon of information', in Carl Mitcham (ed.), *Metaphysics, Epistemology and Technology: Research in Philosophy and Technology*, 19: 79–85 (online at *http://www.capurro.de/ny86.htm*).

Capurro, Rafael (2002) 'The concept of information', in B. Cronin (ed.), *Annual Review of Information Science and Technology*, 27: 343–411 (online at *http://www.capurro.de/infoconcept.html*).

Carey, James (1992) *Communication as Culture: Essays on Media and Society*. New York: Routledge.

Carl, Wolfgang (1994) *Frege's Theory of Sense and Reference: Its Origin and Scope*. Cambridge: Cambridge University Press.

Carnegie Corporation of New York (2004) (online at *http://www.carnegie.org/sub/about/biography.html*).

Cassidy, David (1992) 'Heisenberg, uncertainty and the quantum revolution', *Scientific American*, 266: 106–12.

Castells, Manuel (1989) *The Informational City, Information Technology, Economic Restructuring, and the Urban Regional Process*. Oxford: Basil Blackwell.

Castells, Manuel (1996) *The Information Age: Economy, Society and Culture*, Vol. 1: *The Rise of the Network Society*. Oxford: Blackwell.

Castells, Manuel (1997) *The Information Age: Economy, Society and Culture*, Vol. 2: *The Power of Identity*. Oxford: Blackwell.

Castells, Manuel (1998) *The Information Age: Economy, Society and Culture*, Vol. 3: *End of Millennium*. Oxford: Blackwell.

Chandler, Daniel (1994) 'The Sapir-Whorf hypothesis' (online at *http://www.aber.ac.uk/~dgc/whorf.html*).

Chandler, Daniel (1995) 'Technological or media determinism' (online at *http://www.aber.ac.uk/media/Documents/tecdet/tecdet.html*).

Charnes, George Gilliam (n.d.) 'Museums, archives and libraries: estranged siblings' (online at *http://thedocumentacademy.hum .uit.no/studiegrupper/4.semester/musarchlib.html*).

Cleverdon, C.W. and Keen, E.M. (1966) *Factors Determining the Performance of Indexing Systems*, Vol. 2: *Test Results*. Cranfield: College of Aeronautics.

Cleverdon, C.W., Mills, J. and Keen, E.M. (1966) *Factors Determining the Performance of Indexing Systems*, Vol. 1. Cranfield: College of Aeronautics.

Cohen, Eli (1999) 'Reconceptualizing information systems as a field of the transdiscipline information science: from ugly duckling to swan', *Journal of Computing and Information Technology*, 7 (3): 231–19.

Coleman, J.C. (1988) 'Social capital in the creation of human capital', *American Journal of Sociology*, 94: S95–S120.

Cook, Terry (2000a) 'Archival science and postmodernism: new formulations for old concepts', *Archival Science*, 1 (1): 3–24 (online at *http://www.mybestdocs.com/cook-t-postmod-p1-00 .htm*).

Cook, Terry (2000b) 'Beyond the screen: the records continuum and archival cultural heritage' (online at *http://www .mybestdocs.com/cookt-beyondthescreen-000818.htm*).

Cox, Richard (1996) 'Re-defining electronic records management' (online at *http://xnet.rrc.mb.ca/recmgmt/articles/article1.htm*).

Cox, Richard (1997) 'Millennial thoughts on the education of records professionals', *Records and Information Management Report*, 15 (4), April.

Cox, Richard (1998) 'Do we understand information in the information age?', *Records and Information Management Report*, 14 (3), March.

Cronin, Blaise and Davenport, Elisabeth (1991) *Elements of Information Management*. Metuchen, NJ: Scarecrow Press.

Cunningham, Adrian (1997) 'Ensuring essential evidence: changing archival and records management practices in the electronic recordkeeping era', *Provenance the Web Magazine*, 2 (2) (online at *http://www.netpac.com/provenance/vol2no2/ features/evidence*).

Cunningham, Adrian (1998) *Dynamic Descriptions: Australian Strategies for the Intellectual Control of Records and Record*

Keeping Systems. Presented at Royal Society of Archivists of the Netherlands Symposium, Amsterdam, 23 October.

Danner, R.A. (1998) 'Redefining a profession', *Law Library Journal*, 90 (3): 315–56 (online at *http://www.law.duke.edu/fac/danner/callweb.htm*).

Danziger, J.N. et al. (1982) *Computers and Politics: High Technology in American Local Government.* New York: Columbia University Press.

Darnton, Geoffrey (1992) *Information in the Enterprise: It's More than Technology.* Burlington, MA: Digital Press.

Davies, Bronwyn and Harre, Rom (1990) 'Positioning: the discursive production of selves', *Journal for the Theory of Social Behaviour*, 20 (1): 43–63 (online at *http://www.massey.ac.nz/~alock//position/position.htm*).

Davis, Elisabeth and Hall, Jon (2004) *Measuring Social Capital in Australia.* Canberra: Australian Bureau of Statistics.

Davis, S. and Bodkin, J. (1994) 'The coming of knowledge-based business', *Harvard Business Review*, 72 (5): 165–70.

Davis, William S. (1995) *Management, Information and Systems: An Introduction to Business Information Systems.* Minneapolis/St Paul, MN: West.

Dawkins, Richard (1990) *The Selfish Gene*, 2nd edn. Oxford: Oxford University Press.

Day, R. (1996) 'LIS, method, and postmodern science', *Journal of Education for Library and Information Science*, 37 (4): 317–25.

Derrida, Jacques (1982) *Margins of Philosophy*, trans. Alan Bass. London: Harvester Wheatsheaf.

Dervin, Brenda (1976) 'The everyday information needs of the average citizen: a taxonomy for analysis', in M. Kochen and Donohue (eds), *Information for the Community.* Washington, DC: ALA, pp. 19–38.

Dervin, Brenda (1977) 'Useful theory for librarianship: communication not information', *Drexel Library Quarterly*, 13: 16–32.

Dervin, Brenda (1983) *An Overview of Sense-making Research: Concepts, Methods, and Results to Date.* Presented at International Communication Association Annual Meeting, Dallas, May 1983 (online at *http://edfu.lis.uiuc.edu/allerton/96/w1/Dervin83a.html*).

Dervin, Brenda (1992) 'From the mind's eye of the user: the sense-making qualitative-quantitative methodology', in J.D. Glazier and R.R. Powell (eds), *Qualitative Research in Information Management*. Englewood, CO: Libraries Unlimited Press, pp. 61–84 (online at *http://edfu.lis.uiuc.edu/allerton/96/w1/ Dervin1992a.htm*).

Dervin, Brenda (1995) *Chaos, Order and Sense-making: A Proposed Theory for Information Design* (online at *http://edfu.lis .uiuc.edu/allerton/95/s5/dervin.draft.htm*).

Dervin, Brenda and Nilan, Michael (1986) 'Information needs and uses', *Annual Review of Information Science and Technology*, 21: 3–33.

Design for Social Change (2002, 2004) (online at *http://www.arts .arizona.edu/change/index.html*).

Dick, A.L. (1995) 'Library and information science as a social science: neutral and normative conceptions', *Library Quarterly*, 65 (2): 216–35.

Dodgson, C.L. (Lewis Carroll) (1865, 2000) *Alice's Adventures in Wonderland, and, Through the Looking-glass*. New York: Signet Classics.

Downie, J.S. (1999) 'Jumping off the disintermediation bandwagon: reharmonizing LIS education for the realities of the 21st century' (online at *http://www.lis.edu/jdownie/ alise99/*).

Dreher, Heinz (1997) 'Empowering human cognitive activity through hypertext technology', dissertation (online at *http:// john.curtin.edu.au/theses/public/adt-WCU2000046.121219/*).

Drucker, Peter (1993) *Post-capitalist Society*. New York: Harper Business.

Durrance, J.C. (2000) *KALIPER: What the Field Says about LIS Education at the Dawn of a New Century: An Introduction*. Reston, VA: Association for Library and Information Science Education.

Eckersley, R. (1999) *Quality of Life in Australia: An Analysis of Public Perceptions*, Discussion Paper No. 23. Canberra: Australia Institute.

Ellis, David (1996) *Progress and Problems in Information Retrieval*. London: Library Association Publishing.

Ellul, Jacques (1954, 1964) *The Technological Society*, trans. J. Wilkinson. New York: Knopf.

Emery, F.E. and Trist, E.L. (1965) 'The causal texture of organizational environments', *Human Relations*, 18: 21–32.

Emery, F.E. and Trist, E.L. (1972) *Towards a Social Ecology: Contextual Appreciation of the Future in the Present*. London: Plenum.

Feenberg, Andrew (1991) *Critical Theory of Technology*. Oxford: Oxford University Press.

Fieser, James (ed.) (2004) *Internet Encyclopedia of Philosophy* (online at *http://www.iep.utm.edu/*).

Floriadi, Luciano (2004) 'LIS as applied philosophy of information: a reappraisal', *Library Trends*, 52 (3): 658–65.

Foskett, A.C (1996) *The Subject Approach to Information*, 5th edn. London: Library Association.

Foucault, Michel (1970) *The Order of Things: An Archaeology of the Human Sciences*. London: Tavistock.

Foucault, Michel (1972) *The Archaeology of Knowledge and the Discourse on Language*, trans. A.M. Sheridan Smith. New York: Pantheon Books.

Foucault, Michel (1984) *The Foucault Reader*, ed. Paul Rabinow. London: Penguin.

Frohmann, Bernd (1992) 'The ethics of information science theory', *Information Democracy: Creating an Agenda for Action: Power and Control Issues in the US*, 55th ASIS Annual Meeting, Pittsburgh, 26–29 October (online at *http://www.fims.uwo.ca/people/faculty/frohmann/Ethics.htm*).

Frohmann, Bernd (1994) 'Discourse analysis as a research method in library and information science', *Library and Information Science Research*, 16: 119–38.

Frohmann, Bernd (1995) 'Taking information policy beyond information science: applying the Actor Network Theory', in Hope A. Olsen and Dennis B. Ward (eds), *Connectedness: Information, Systems, People, Organizations: Proceedings of the 23rd Annual Conference of the Canadian Association for Information Science*, 7–10 June. Edmonton: University of Alberta.

Frohmann, Bernd (1997) 'Taking information policy beyond information science: applying the actor-network theory' (online at *http://www.ualberta.ca/dept/slis/cais/frohmann.htm*).

Frohmann, Bernd (2000) 'The politics of postmodern information science' (online at *http://www.instruct.uwo.ca/faculty/Frohmann/pomoIS.htm*).

Galvin, Thomas J. (1995) 'Convergence or divergence in education for the information professions: an opinion paper', *Bulletin of the American Society for Information Science*, August–September.

Gerbner, G. (1983) 'The importance of being critical – in one's own fashion', *Journal of Communication*, 33 (3): 355–62.

Gibbons, Michael et al. (1994) *The New Production of Knowledge: The Dynamics of Science and Research in Contemporary Societies*. London: Sage.

Giddens, Anthony (1990) *The Consequences of Modernity*. Stanford, CA: Stanford University Press.

Gililand-Swetland, Anne (2000) *Enduring Paradigm, New Opportunities: The Value of the Archival Perspective in the Digital Environment*. Washington, DC: Council on Library and Information Resources (online at *http://www.clir.org/pubs/reports/reports.html*).

Goldman, Alvin (1999) *Knowledge in a Social World*. Oxford: Oxford University Press.

Gorman, G.E. and Corbitt, B.J. (2002) 'Core competencies in information management education', *New Library World*, 103 (1182–3): 436–45.

Hacking, Ian (2001) *The Social Construction of What?* Cambridge, MA: Harvard University Press.

Hamlyn, D.W. (1967) 'History of epistemology', in P. Edwards (ed.), *The Encyclopedia of Philosophy*, Vol. 3. New York: Macmillan, pp. 8–38.

Haraway, Donna (1991) *Simians, Cyborgs and Women: The Reinvention of Nature*. London: Free Association.

Harter, Stephen P. (1996) 'Variations in relevance assessments and the measurements of retrieval effectiveness', *Journal of the American Society for Information Science*, 47: 137–49.

Hayek, F.A. (1956) 'The dilemma of specialization', in L.D. White (ed.), *The State of the Social Sciences*. Chicago: Chicago University Press, pp. 462–73.

Heald, Carolyn (1995) 'Are we collecting the "right stuff"?', *Archivaria*, 40 (Fall): 182–8.

Heidegger, Martin (1977) *The Question Concerning Technology*, trans. W. Lovitt. New York: Harper & Row.

Heim, Michael (1993) *The Metaphysics of Virtual Reality*. Oxford: Oxford University Press.

Hekman, Susan J. (1990) *Gender and Knowledge: Elements of a Postmodern Feminism*. Cambridge: Polity Press.

Hert, Carol (1997) *Understanding Information Retrieval Interactions: Theoretical and Practical Implications*. Greenwich, CT: Ablex.

Hjørland, Birger (2000a) 'Library and information science: practice, theory and philosophical basis', *Information Processing and Management*, 36: 501–31.

Hjørland, Birger (2000b) 'Documents, memory institutions and information science', *Journal of Documentation*, 56 (1): 27–41.

Holtham, Clive (1996) 'Collaboration, knowledge and action', in *Proceedings of 'Nouveaux modes de travail et de création de richesses sous l'influence des réseaux d'ordinateurs'*. Paris: Euro-technopolis Institute and ESCP.

IFLA (2000) 'Guidelines for professional library/information educational programs, 2000' (online at *http://www.ifla.org/VII/s23/bulletin/guidelines.htm*).

Information Policy Advisory Council (IPAC) (1997) *A National Policy Framework for Structural Adjustment within the New Commonwealth of Information: A Report to the Minister for Communications and the Arts*. Canberra: AGPO.

Ingwersen, Peter (1992) *Information Retrieval Interaction*. London: Taylor Graham.

Jacobs, Jane (1961) *The Death and Life of Great American Cities*. New York: Random Books.

James, William (1907) *A New Name for Some Old Ways of Thinking*. New York: Longmans, Green.

Jarvelin, Kalervo and Vakkari, Pertti (1991) 'Content analysis of research articles in library and information science', *Library and Information Science Research*, 12: 395–421.

Jonassen, David (2001) *Bulletin of the American Society for Information Science and Technology*, April/May: 15.

Jordan, Glenn and Weedon, Chris (1995) *Cultural Politics: Class, Gender, Race and the Postmodern World.* Oxford, Blackwell.

Julien, Heidi (1996) 'Trends in the recent information needs and uses literature: a content analysis' (online at *http://www .ualberta.ca/dept/slis/cais/julien.htm*).

Julien, Heidi (1999) 'Constructing "users" in library and information science', *Aslib Proceedings*, 51 (6): 206–13.

Julien, Heidi and Duggan, L.J. (2000) 'A longitudinal analysis of the information needs and uses literature', *Library and Information Science Research*, 22 (3): 291–309.

KALIPER (2000) *The Kellogg-ALISE Information Professions and Education Reform Project Report* (online at *http:// www.alise.org/publications/kaliper.pdf*).

Kando, Noriko (1994) 'Information concepts reexamined', *International Forum on Information and Documentation*, 19 (2): 20–4.

Kaufer, David S. and Carely, Kathleen M. (1993) *Communication at a Distance: The Influence of Print on Sociocultural Organization and Change.* Hillsdale, NJ: Lawrence Erlbaum.

Kaye, J. (2000) 'The greying of the teacher librarian ALIA conference' (online at *http://www.alia.org.au/conferences/alia2000/ proceedings/jan.kaye.html*).

Kellner, Douglas (1999) 'Globalization and the postmodern turn' (online at *http://www.gseis.ucla.edu/courses/ed253a/dk/ GLOBPM.htm*).

Kim, B. (2001) 'Social constructivism', in M. Orey (ed.), *Emerging Perspectives on Learning, Teaching, and Technology* (online at *http://www.coe.uga.edu/epitt/SocialConstructivism.htm*).

Kling, Rob (1994) 'Reading "all about" computerization: how genre conventions shape non-fiction social analysis', *The Information Society*, 10 (3): 147–72 (online at *http://www.ic .suci.edu/kling/read94a.html*).

Kling, Rob (1999) 'What is social informatics and why does it matter?', *D-Lib Magazine*, 5 (1), January.

Kling, Rob (2001) 'Social informatics', *Encyclopedia of LIS*. Kingston upon Thames: Kluwer (online at *http://www.slis .indiana.edu/SI/si2001.html*).

Kling, Rob and McKim, Geoffrey (1999) *Not Just a Matter of Time: Field Differences and the Shaping of Electronic Media in*

Supporting Scientific Communication, CSI Working Paper No. WP-99-02 (online at *http://www.slis.indiana.edu/CSI/WP/wp99_02B.html*).

Knight, J. and de Wit, H. (1995) 'Strategies for internationalisation of higher education: historical and conceptual perspectives', in H. de Wit (ed.), *Strategies for Internationalisation of Higher Education*. Amsterdam: EAIE.

Kofler, Angelika (1998) 'Digital Europe 1998: policies, technological development and implementation of the emerging information society', *Innovation*, 11 (1).

Korzybski, Alfred (1994) *Science and Sanity: An Introduction to non-Aristotelian Systems and General Semantics*, 5th edn. London: Institute of General Semantics.

Kuhlthau, Carol C. (1991) 'Inside the search process: information seeking from the user's perspective', *Journal of the American Society for Information Science*, 42: 361–71.

Kuhlthau, Carol C. (1993) *Seeking Meaning: A Process Approach to Library and Information Services*. Norwood, NJ: Ablex.

Kuhn, Thomas S. (1962) *The Structure of Scientific Revolutions*. Chicago: University of Chicago Press.

Lancaster, F.W. (1984) 'Implications for library and information science education', *Library Trends*, 32 (3): 337–48.

Landow, George P. (1992) *Hypertext: The Convergence of Contemporary Critical Theory and Technology*. London: Johns Hopkins University Press.

Latour, Bruno and Woolgar, Steve (1986) *Laboratory Life: The Construction of Scientific Facts*. Princeton, NJ: Princeton University Press.

Lemert, Charles (1990) 'The uses of French structuralisms in sociology', in G. Ritzer (ed.), *Frontiers of Social Theory: New Syntheses*. New York: Columbia University Press.

Levy, David M. (1995) 'Cataloging in the digital order' (online at *http://www.csdl.tamu.edu/DL95/papers/levy/levy.html*).

Lincoln, Y. and Guba, E. (1985) *Naturalistic Inquiry*. New York: Sage.

Lubar, Steven (1993) *InfoCulture*. Boston: Houghton Mifflin.

Luhmann, Niklas (1990) 'Societal complexity and public opinion', in *Political Theory in the Welfare State*, trans. John Bednarz. Berlin: De Gruyter, pp. 203–18.

Lycan, W.G. (2000) *Philosophy of Language: A Contemporary Introduction*. New York: Routledge.

Lynch, Aaron (1996) *Thought Contagion*. New York: Basic Books.

Lyon, David (1988) *The Information Society: Issues and Illusions*. Cambridge: Polity Press.

Lyotard, Jean-François (1979, 1984) *La condition postmoderne: rapport sur le savoir* (*The Postmodern Condition: A Report on Knowledge*), trans. Geoff Bennington and Brian Massumi. Minnesota: University of Minnesota Press.

Machlup, Fritz (1962) *The Production and Distribution of Knowledge in the United States*. Princeton, NJ: Princeton University Press.

Machlup, Fritz (1980, 1982, 1984) *Knowledge: Its Creation, Distribution and Economic Significance*, 3 vols. Princeton, NJ: Princeton University Press.

Machlup, Fritz and Mansfield, Una (eds) (1983) *The Study of Information: Interdisciplinary Messages*. New York: John Wiley & Sons.

Malhotra, Yogesh (1997) 'Knowledge management in inquiring organizations', in *Proceedings of 3rd Americas Conference on Information Systems* (Philosophy of Information Systems Mini-track), Indianapolis, 15–17 August, pp. 293–5.

Manley, W. (1991) 'Professional survival: it's academic', *Wilson Library Bulletin*, 65 (6): 79–81.

Mannheim, Karl (1936, 1968) *Ideology and Utopia: An Introduction to the Sociology of Knowledge*, trans. Louis Wirth and Edward Shils. New York: Harcourt, Brace & World.

Marchionini, Gary (1995) *Information Seeking in Electronic Environments*. New York: Cambridge University Press.

Markus, M.L. and Robey, D. (1988) 'Information technology and organizational change: causal structure in theory and research', *Management Science*, 34 (5): 583–98.

McInnis, C., Hartley, R. and Anderson, M. (2001) *What Did You Do with Your Science Degree?* Australian Council of Deans of Science (ACDS) (online at *http://www.acds.edu.au/occas.htm*).

McKechnie, Lynne, Pettigrew, Karen E. and Joyce, Steven L. (2001) 'The origins and contextual use of theory in human information behaviour research', *The New Review of Infor-*

mation Behaviour Research: Studies of Information Seeking in Context, 2: 47–65.

Middleton, Michael (2002) Information Management: A Consolidation of Operations, Analysis and Strategy. Wagga Wagga: CSU Centre for Information Studies.

Mizzaro, Stefano (1997) 'Relevance: the whole history', Journal of the American Society of Information Science, 28 (9): 810–32.

Mosco, Vincent (1992) 'Dinosaurs alive: toward a political economy of information', Canadian Journal of Information Science/Revue Canadienne des Sciences de l'Information, 17 (1): 41–51.

Mosco, Vincent (1996) The Political Economy of Communication: Rethinking and Renewal. London: Sage.

Murphy, Julia (n.d.) 'The implications of name changes for library and information management schools' (online at (http://www.crowbold.com/homepage/topic4.htm).

Myburgh, Sue (2000) 'The convergence of information management and information technology', Information Management Quarterly, April.

Myburgh, Sue (2003) 'Following the Phoenicians: RIM in a globalised future', Information Management Journal, September/October, 37 (5).

Myburgh, Sue and Nimon, Maureen (2001) 'Theory with praxis: a rationale for education in information', International Conference for Library and Information Science Educators in the Asia Pacific Region (ICLISE 2001), 11–12 June, Petaling Jaya, Malaysia (online at http://www.iiu.edu.my/iclise).

Nahl, Diane (1996) 'The user-centred revolution: 1970–1995', in Encyclopedia of Microcomputers, 19: 143–99 (online at http://www2.hawaii.edu/~nahl/articles/user/user1toend_toc.html).

National Archives of Australia (2004) Glossary of Recordkeeping Terminology (online at http://www.naa.gov.au/recordkeeping/rkpubs/recordkeepingglossary.html).

Neill, S.D. (1992) Dilemmas in the Study of Information: Exploring the Boundaries of Information Science. New York: Greenwood.

Nelson, Ted. (n.d.) (online at http://en.wikipedia.org/wiki/Intertwingularity).

Neuss, Christian and Kent, Robert E. (1995) 'Conceptual analysis of resource meta-information' (online at *http://www.igd.fhg.de/archive/1995_www95/papers/94/www3.html*).

Newby, Gregory B. (1993) 'Towards Navigation for Information Retrieval' (unpublished dissertation) (online at *http://www.petascale.org/papers/diss.txt*).

Nilan, Michael S. et al. (2004) 'Virtual communities on the Web: facilitating and hindering users' cognitive movement' (online at *http://web.syr.edu/~iguzmand/nilanetal04.pdf*).

Nissani, Moti (1997) 'Ten cheers for interdisciplinarity: the case for interdisciplinary knowledge and research', *Social Science Journal*, 34 (2): 201–16 (online at *http://www.is.wayne.edu/mnissani/PAGEPUB/10CHEERS.HTM*).

Nonaka, Ikujiro and Takeuchi, Hirotaka (1995) *The Knowledge-Creating Company: How Japanese Companies Create the Dynamics of Innovation*. Oxford: Oxford University Press.

Oettinger, Anthony G. (1980) 'Information resources: knowledge and power in the 21st century', *Science*, 209: 191–8.

Oppenheim, Charles, Stenson, Joan and Wilson, Richard M.S. (2003) 'Studies on information as an asset 1: definitions', *Journal of Information Science*, 29 (3): 159–66.

Ostler, Larry J. and Dahlin, Therrin C. (1995) 'Library education: setting or rising sun?', *American Libraries*, 26 (7): 683–6.

Ostler, L.J., Dahlin, T.C. and Willardson, J.D. (1995) *The Closing of American Library Schools: Problems and Opportunities*. Westport, CT: Greenwood Press.

Pacey, Arnold (1997) *Technology in World Civilization: A Thousand-Year History*. Cambridge, MA: MIT Press.

Pahre, Robert (1996) 'Patterns of knowledge communities in the social sciences', *Library Trends*, 44 (2): 204–26.

Palmquist, R.A. and Kim, K.S. (1998) 'Modeling the users of information systems: some theories and methods', in H. Iyer (ed.), *Electronic Resources: Use and User Behavior*. Binghampton, NY: Haworth Press.

Parker, Edwin B. and Paisley, William J. (1966) *Patterns of Adult Information Seeking*. Palo Alto, CA: Stanford University Press.

Parsons, Talcott (1968) 'Professions', *International Encyclopedia of Social Science*, 12: 536.

Pearce-Moses, Richard (2004) *A Glossary of Archival and Records Terminology* (online at *http://www.archivists.org/glossary/*).

Pierce, Sidney (1992) 'Dead Germans and the theory of librarianship', *American Libraries*, 23: 641.

Pinker, Steven (2002) *The Blank Slate: The Modern Denial of Human Nature*. New York: Viking Penguin.

Pippin, Robert (1995) 'On the notion of technology as ideology', in A. Feenberg and A. Hannay (eds), *Technology and the Politics of Knowledge*. Indiana: Indiana University Press, pp. 43–59.

Plant, Sadie (1997) *Zeros and Ones: Digital Women and the New Technoculture*. New York: Doubleday.

Popper, Karl (1973) 'Indeterminism is not enough', *Encounter*, 40 (4): 20–6.

Poster, Mark (1990) *The Mode of Information: Poststructuralism and Social Context*. Chicago: University of Chicago Press.

Poster, Mark (1995) 'Cyberdemocracy: Internet and the public sphere' (online at *http://www.hnet.uci.edu/mposter/writings/democ.html*).

Potter, Jonathan (1996) *Representing Reality: Discourse, Rhetoric and Social Construction*. Thousand Oaks, CA: Sage.

Putnam, Hilary (1974) 'The "corroboration" of theories', in P.A. Schilpp (ed.), *The Philosophy of Karl Popper*, Vol. I. Peru, IL: Open Court, pp. 221–40.

Putnam, Robert D. (1995) 'Bowling alone: America's declining social capital', *Journal of Democracy*, July.

Putnam, Robert D. (2000) *Bowling Along: The Collapse and Revival of American Community*. New York: Simon & Schuster.

Radford, Gary P. (1998) 'Flaubert, Foucault, and the Bibliothèque fantastique: toward a postmodern epistemology for library science', *Library Trends*, 46 (4): 616–35.

Rayward, Boyd W. (1994) 'Some schemes for restructuring and mobilising information in documents: a historical perspective', *Information Processing and Management*, 20 (2): 163–75.

Rheingold, Howard (1993) *The Virtual Community: Homesteading on the Electronic Frontier*. Cambridge, MA: MIT Press.

Risager, Karen (1999) 'Language and culture: disconnection and reconnection', in Torben Vestergaard (ed.), *Language, Culture and Identity*. Aalborg: Aalborg University Press, pp. 83–98.

Robbins-Carter, J. and Seavey, C.A. (1986) 'The Master's degree: basic preparation for professional practice', *Library Trends*, 34 (4): 561–80.

Robins, Kevin and Webster, Frank (1997) 'From ICTs to information: changing conceptions of the Information Age', in *Times of the Technoculture: From the Information Society to the Virtual Life*. New York: Routledge.

Rosenbaum, Howard (1993) 'Information use environments and structuration: towards an integration of Taylor and Giddens', in *Proceedings of the 6th Annual Meeting of the American Society for Information Science*, 30: 235–45.

Rosenfeld, Lou and Morville, Peter (2002) *Information Architecture for the World Wide Web: Designing Large-scale Web Sites*, 2nd edn. New York: O'Reilly.

Ross, Andrew (1989) *No Respect: Intellectuals and Popular Culture*. London: Routledge.

Ross, Kelly L. (1999) 'Meaning and the problem of universals' (online at *http://www.friesian.com/universl.htm*).

Rowley, Jennifer (1999) 'In pursuit of the discipline of information management', *New Review of Information and Library Research*, 65–77.

Rowley, Jennifer (2003) 'Knowledge management – the new librarianship? From custodians of history to gatekeepers to the future', *Library Management*, 24 (8–9): 433–40.

Saffo, Paul (1997) 'Are you machine wise?', *Harvard Business Review*, September/October: 28–30.

Said, Eward (1986) 'Orientalism and the October War: the shattered myths', in Baha abu-Laban and Faith T. Zeadey (eds), *Arabs in America: Myths and Realities*. Wilmette, IL: Medina University Press.

Saracevic, Tefko (1994) 'Closing of library schools in North America: what role accreditation?', *Libri*, 44: 190–200.

Saussure, F. (1983) *Cours de linguistique generale* (*Course in General Linguistics*, first published 1916). London: Duckworth.

Sawyer, Steve and Rosenbaum, Howard (2000) 'Social informatics in the information sciences: current activities and emerging directions', *Information Science*, 3 (2): 89–95.

Schamber, Linda, Eisenberg, Michael B. and Nilan, Michael S. (1990) 'A re-examination of relevance: toward a dynamic, situational definition', *Information Processing and Management*, 26 (6): 755–76.

Schiller, Herbert I. (1989) 'Information for what kind of society?', in Jerry L. Salvaggio (ed.), *The Information Society: Economy, Social, and Structural Issues*. Mahwah, NJ: Lawrence Erlbaum Associates.

Schrader, A.M. (1983) *Toward a Theory of Library and Information Science*, 2 vols. Ann Arbor, MI: University Microfilm International.

Seely-Brown, John (1997) 'The human factor', *Information Strategy*, December 1996–January 1997.

Shannon, Claude (1948) 'The mathematical theory of communication', *Bell System Technical Journal*, July and October, 27: 379–423 and 623–56.

Shepherd, G.J. (1993) 'Building a discipline of communication', *Journal of Communication*, 43 (3): 83–91.

Shera, Jesse (1961) 'Social epistemology, general semantics, and librarianship', *Wilson Library Bulletin*, 35: 767–70.

Shera, Jesse (1970) 'The library and knowledge', *Sociological Foundations of Librarianship*. New York: Asia Publishing House, pp. 82–110.

Sheridan, Michel (1980) *Foucault: The Will to Truth*. New York: Tavistock.

Simmel, Georg (1976) *Georg Simmel: Sociologist and European*, ed. P.A. Lawrence. Sunbury-on-Thames: Nelson.

Slack, Jennifer Daryl and Fejes, Fred (1987) *The Ideology of the Information Age*. Norwood, NJ: Ablex.

Snow, C.P. (1964) 'The two cultures', in *The Two Cultures: and, A Second Look*. Cambridge: Cambridge University Press, pp. 1–51.

Solow, Robert M. (1987) 'We'd better watch out', *New York Times Book Review*, July: 36.

Sonnenwald, D.H. (1999) 'Evolving perspectives of human information behaviour: contexts, situations, social networks and information horizons', in T.D. Wilson and D.K. Allen (eds), *Exploring the Contexts of Information Behaviour: Proceedings of the 2nd International Conference on Information Needs, Use and Seeking in Different Contexts*. London: Taylor Graham.

Spellerberg, A. (2001) *Framework for the Measurement of Social Capital in New Zealand*, Research and Analytical Report 14. Wellington: Statistics New Zealand.

Steemson, Michael (1999) 'Cricket, rugby and records management ... we've set the standard' (online at *http://www.caldeson.com/crimby.html*).

Stieg, M.F. (1992) *Change and Challenge in Library and Information Science Education*. Chicago: American Library Association.

Strati, Antonio (1998) 'Organizational symbolism as a social construction: a perspective from the sociology of knowledge', *Human Relations*, 51 (11): 1379–99.

Sutton, S.A. (1999) 'The Panda Syndrome II: innovation, discontinuous change, and LIS education', *Journal of Education for Library and Information Science*, 40 (4): 247–62.

Tapscott, Don (1999) *Growing Up Digital: The Rise of the Net Generation*. New York: McGraw-Hill.

Taylor, Robert (1972) *The Making of a Library: The Academic Library in Transition*. New York: Becker & Hayes.

Tenkasie, Ramkrishnan V. and Boland, Richard J. (1998) 'Exploring knowledge diversity in knowledge intensive firms: a new role for information systems', *Journal of Systematic Knowledge Management* (online at *http://www.tlainc.com/article4.htm*).

Thomassen, Theo (1999) 'The development of archival science and its European dimension' (online at *http://www.daz.hr/arhol/thomassen.htm*).

Thompson Klein, Julie (1996) *Crossing Boundaries: Knowledge, Disciplinarities and Interdisciplinarities*. Charlottesville, VA: University Press of Virginia.

Tuominen, K., Talja, S. and Savolainen, R. (2002) 'Discourse, cognition and reality: towards a social constructionist metatheory for library and information science', in H. Bruce, R. Fidel, P. Ingwersen and P. Vakkari (eds), *Emerging Frameworks and Methods COLIS 4: Proceedings of the Fourth International Conference on Conceptions of Library and Information Science, Seattle, July 21–25, 2002*. Norwood, NJ: Libraries Unlimited, pp. 271–83.

Turchin, Valentin (1977) *The Phenomenon of Science*. New York: Columbia University Press.

Upward, Frank (1997) 'Structuring the records continuum, part two: structuration theory and recordkeeping', *Archives and Manuscripts*, 25 (1): 10–35.

Upward, Frank (2000) 'Modelling the continuum as paradigm shift in recordkeeping and archiving processes and beyond: a personal reflection', *Records Management Journal*, 10 (3): 115–39.

Van House, Nancy A. and Sutton, S.A. (1996) 'The panda syndrome: an ecology of LIS education', *Journal of Education for Library and Information Science* (online at *http://sims .berkeley.edu/~vanhouse/panda.html*).

Vickery, Brian and Vickery, Alina (1992) *Information Science in Theory and Practice*, rev. edn. East Grinstead: Bowker-Saur.

Vogel, Steven (1995) 'New science, new nature: the Habermas-Marcuse debate revisited', in Andrew Feenberg and Alastair Hannay (eds), *Technology and the Politics of Knowledge*. Bloomington, IN: Indiana University Press.

Voloshinov, V.N. (1994) 'Critique of Sausserian linguistics', in Pam Morris (ed.), *Bakhtin Reader*. London: Edward Arnold.

Waples, Douglas (1931) 'The Graduate Library School at Chicago', *Library Quarterly*, 1: 26–36.

Weaver, Warren and Shannon, Claude E. (1949, 1963) *The Mathematical Theory of Communication*. Urbana, IL: University of Illinois Press.

Webster's Third New International Dictionary of the English Language.

Westbrook, Lynn (1999) *Interdisciplinary Information Seeking in Women's Studies*. Jefferson, NC: McFarland.

White, Herbert S. (1987) 'The funding of corporate libraries: old myths and new problems', *Special Libraries*, 78: 155–61.

White, Herbert S. (1995) *At the Crossroads: Librarians on the Information Superhighway*. Englewood, CO: Libraries Unlimited.

White, Leslie (1949) *The Science of Culture: A Study of Man and Civilization*. New York: Grove Press.

Willard, Patricia and Mychalyn, Janette (1998) 'New information management work in a changing world: an Australian survey',

International Journal of Information Management, 18 (5): 315–27.

Wilson, Patrick (1994) 'Communication efficiency in research and development', *Journal of the American Society for Information Science*, 44 (7): 376–82.

Wilson, Patrick (1995) 'Unused relevant information in research and development', *Journal of the American Society for Information Science*, 46 (1): 45–51.

Wilson, T.D. (2000) 'Curriculum and catastrophe: change in professional education' (online at *http://www.alise.org/nondiscuss/conf00_Wilson-Curriculum.htm*).

Wilson, T.D. (2002) 'The nonsense of "knowledge management"', *Information Research*, 8 (1), October (online at *http://information.net/ir/8-1/paper144.html*).

WorDiq.com (2004) 'Definitions' (online at *http://www.wordiq.com/*).

World Bank (2004) 'How is social capital measured?' (online at *http://www1.worldbank.org/prem/poverty/scapital/SChowmeas1.htm#measurement_tools*).

Young, Peter R. (1996) 'Librarianship: a changing profession', *Daedalus*, 125 (4): 103–25.

Zipf, G.K. (1949) *Human Behavior and the Principle of Least Effort*. Cambridge, MA: Addison-Wesley.

Index

Printed in the United States
117302LV00002B/57/A